AUTHENTICITY

IN LEADERSHIP

**A Change
Management
Fable**

DR. DAVID BROWN, JR.

Authenticity in Leadership
A Change Management Fable
by David Brown, Jr.

1. BUS071000   BUSINESS & ECONOMICS / Leadership
2. BUS041000   BUSINESS & ECONOMICS / Management
3. BUS103000   BUSINESS & ECONOMICS / Organizational Development

ISBN (paperback): 979-8-88636-074-5
ISBN (hardcover): 979-8-88636-075-2
ISBN (ebook): 979-8-88636-076-9

Library of Congress Control Number: 2026902679

Cover design by Kolton Durkin and Lewis Agrell

Printed in the United States of America

Authority Publishing
13389 Folsom Blvd #300-256
Folsom, CA 95630
800-877-1097
www.AuthorityPublishing.com

"This is exactly the book needed to bring the very timely concept of workplace and leadership authenticity into public realization and action. As we're increasingly pummeled in our work lives with false information, profiteering, self-promotion, narcissism, and AI-generated clutter, this book tells a captivating tale that emphasizes the importance of being authentic as individuals as well as collectively as organizations. Through deft storytelling, David Brown, Jr. brings authentic leadership to life in a way that's far more compelling than the standard business press book. There's no one more qualified to simultaneously weave this tale into practical wisdom; David Brown, Jr. is not only a practitioner of authenticity, he is a scholar who has furthered research on the concept in a deep and meaningful way."

– Lynne Andersson,
Associate Professor Business,
Society and Ethics, Temple University

"In an environment where leaders are often asked to drive transformation at speed, authenticity becomes the anchor that keeps people aligned and engaged. *Authenticity in Leadership* offers a powerful reminder that real change begins with self-awareness and the courage to lead with purpose. Through an engaging story, David captures what many leaders learn through experience—that authenticity isn't a soft skill, it's a strategic advantage."

– Darrell Fincher-Crusan,
Head of Human Resources,
Octapharma Plasma

"The greatest risk to any change initiative isn't the strategy; it's the gap between who a leader is and how they actually show up. Real leadership doesn't require a mask—it requires a mirror. When we shift our shape just to make others comfortable, skepticism breeds and trust stalls. To lead others through transformation, you must first connect your own authenticity to the mission, because a team will never follow a leader who hasn't journeyed into themselves first. If you need a place to start, this book is it!"

– Barbara Caramés,
Strategic Business Performance Leader,
Advocate for Authentic Leadership

"*Authenticity in Leadership* is written as a fable, but the situations will feel very familiar to anyone who has led change inside a real organization. The story brings to life a powerful idea: that authenticity is a leadership capability that can transform teams, cultures, and outcomes.

One of the book's strongest contributions is its simple but powerful framework linking individual authenticity, collective authenticity, and the results organizations ultimately produce. The message is clear: when leaders align values, behaviors, and purpose, trust grows and change becomes possible."

– Caroline Faulkner,
Executive Mindset Coach,
Former CEO

"I've had the privilege of knowing Dr. David Brown, Jr. for over 15 years, and throughout that time, he has consistently demonstrated a commitment to leadership that goes beyond getting the work done—he is deeply focused on making teams better. In this book, David elevates the concept of 'authenticity' beyond a cultural buzzword, offering a practical framework for developing the capabilities of individuals, teams, and organizations."

– James B. Rosseau, Sr.,
Founder, The Corelink Solution
CEO, Holy Culture

"When leaders align purpose with role, both people and performance flourish. This book brings that insight to life. Through a story punctuated by reflective date-night conversations, this fable demonstrates how authenticity, when practiced intentionally, becomes a catalyst for trust, engagement, and sustainable change. Drawing on a deep understanding and research on organizational life and the human experience of leadership, Dr. David Brown, Jr. offers a thoughtful and credible guide for leaders who want to create workplaces where meaning, alignment, and results coexist."

– Bucky Fairfax, DBA
Executive Vice President and
Chief Human Resources Officer,
RTI International

"Here is a fable that's more reality than it is fiction. The illustrations make the dynamics of authenticity come to life as the characters and frameworks dance across the pages."

– Marcus Collins,
bestselling author of
For the Culture and Professor
at the University of Michigan

Table of Contents

Introduction

As organizations face more disruption than at any other time in recent history, leading through change is increasingly complex. Externally, there's groundbreaking technological innovation, shifts in global markets, and even geopolitical uncertainty. Internally, leaders must balance business objectives with maintaining organizational alignment, developing the workforce, and helping employees make meaning of their work. Because leaders are understandably stretched thin as they attempt to deliver on those promises in a fluctuating marketplace, it's easy for them to lose sight of who they truly are. They no longer know their true, authentic selves. And when authenticity disappears, they can't perform at their best. So, everyone suffers, not just the leader.

The word "authenticity" has been in the lexicon for years. And though people covet it, not much is taught about the journey to authenticity or the positive impact authenticity has on leadership. This book presents authenticity as not only a way of being but as a solution for many of our organizational and societal challenges.

It is easy to think of authenticity as simply being true to yourself, but in organizational life, that reality is much more nuanced. Leaders often feel caught between who they want to be and who they are expected to be within the context of the organization. That natural tension exists for most. And when the stakes are high — a major transformation, a difficult culture shift, a business model pivot — authenticity can easily become an afterthought.

But what happens if we lean into our own personal authenticity during these challenging times? What exists on the other side of that experience?

While exploring answers to these questions, this book begins with a bold research-based premise: Authenticity can be a catalyst for transformational change. In fact, because authenticity is an innately human characteristic, I believe it is a foundational capability that can influence and improve all organizational capabilities, including change management.

Why a Fable

Rather than offer another dense textbook on leadership theory, this book takes the form of a story. Stories have a way of sneaking past our defenses. They invite us to see ourselves through the lens of characters that come alive in our minds and hearts. In a fable, we can watch leaders wrestle with difficult decisions, navigate politics, recover from mistakes, and rediscover courage. All the while, we learn from the story by integrating the lessons with our own memories and personal observations.

The story you are about to read is fiction. None of the characters, including our protagonist and highly authentic leader, Oscar, are real people. And yet, every situation and scenario they encounter is drawn from some level of real-world experience. Fables have an engaging way of introducing complex lessons that allow you, the reader, to see your own experiences and challenges through the lens of the characters.

Authenticity is a complex phenomenon. This book presents a simplistic view of authenticity. Moving away from the linear action steps you'll find in a conventional business book, this book shows how each leader's journey to becoming more authentic is a unique experience. The fable format facilitates this by offering a completely flexible way of understanding and interpreting the concepts presented.

The Central Theme

Everyone operates at their own authenticity level. Organizations have their own authenticity, too. We sometimes call that culture. The products and services the organization produces also have their own authenticity that reflects the organization's people, processes, technology, and systems. To make sense of this, I describe authenticity through three lenses:

1. **Individual Authenticity** — This is the alignment level between a person's internal thoughts, values, and beliefs and their actions and behaviors. The more aligned those inner and outer worlds feel, the higher the level of authenticity. For example, a person who is in flow and operating with a sense of freedom in a meeting is doing what they think and feel. That is high individual authenticity. On the contrary, if that same person feels angst about expressing themselves, maybe due to fear or judgment, they experience low individual authenticity.

2. **Collective Authenticity** — This term describes how aligned a group's shared thoughts, values, and beliefs are with the expected actions and behaviors that define belonging. An example of collective authenticity is an organization's culture or how work gets done there. When a person joins a new organization, they learn to assimilate into the new culture. They are, in essence, moving from one collective authenticity to another.

3. **Manifested Authenticity** — This represents the products, services, or outcomes that emerge from the individuals and collectives. These, too, carry fingerprints of authenticity that reflect the creators. Wegmans, a grocery chain known for superior customer service that always ranks at the top of Best Workplace and Best Supermarket lists, is a great example. Several of its core values, including caring for people and the planet and demonstrating high standards in all actions, are critical to its superior customer service mission. Its stated mission, in fact, is almost the definition of organizationally manifested authenticity: "At Wegmans, we believe that good people, working toward a common goal, can accomplish anything they set out to do." If the company's mission or core values were to change, the output or service level would also change significantly.

When individuals feel authentic, energy flows. When organizations nurture collective authenticity, trust deepens. And when both come together, their creations carry a unique resonance that customers, employees, and stakeholders can feel.

Authenticity is constantly tested as the organizational context changes. Transformation and a new vision of the future can trigger resistance in some, while others embrace it. That resistance is a natural signal that we don't feel aligned. On the other side of that is resonance — that sense of alignment. Gaining sufficient momentum towards resonance is key to making change happen. Moving people, teams, and organizations from resistance to resonance is at the heart of leading through change with high authenticity. That is what this book is about.

What You Can Expect

As you read, you will notice that this is not a how-to manual. I won't give you a rigid set of steps guaranteed to deliver success. Instead, you'll find a story to reflect on and frameworks that can be adapted to your leadership. You will recognize familiar dynamics:

- An organization that resists change because past successes suggest that doing things "the way we've always done them" will still work in a dramatically different environment

- A senior leadership team that is not aligned with the organization's priorities

- Leaders who want a new future but feel disempowered or not supported in creating that future

- New leaders who have ideas but are often not heard

- Employees who desperately want to believe in the future but carry scars from the past

- Leaders torn between loyalty to colleagues and responsibility to shareholders

- Teams that celebrate mediocre results because they are exhausted by failed change efforts

- The presence of fear and its paralyzing consequences

And woven throughout, you will see how authenticity can shift these dynamics. You'll discover how a transparent conversation can break down fear, a leader's vulnerability can inspire trust, and aligning values with actions can unlock new possibilities.

By the end of the book, you will not only have walked with Oscar and his colleagues through their journey of change, but you will also have language, frameworks, and tools to apply in your own leadership. You will understand authenticity not as a vague aspiration but as a tangible capability you can practice.

A Note to You, the Reader

This book is written for leaders at every level. You may be a first-time manager learning how to balance relationships with results or a senior executive facing the weight of shareholder expectations. Perhaps you're someone outside formal leadership who nonetheless influences people and culture every day. *Whoever you are, I invite you to read slowly.* Pause when something resonates. Notice when you feel your own resistance. Pay attention to which character you identify with most and why.

I also encourage you to read the brief leadership bios in the Appendix before moving to Chapter 1. This will give you a sense of the main characters' personalities.

In addition, here are some questions to carry with you:

- Where do I feel most authentic in my leadership today?
- When do I feel resistance or a lack of alignment?
- How might I lead in a way that creates more resonance for myself and others?
- What would it look like for authenticity to be my greatest capability, not just my aspiration?

An Invitation

As you turn the page to Chapter 1, remember this: The journey towards highly authentic leadership is taken one step at a time. This book might be your first step. Know that leading with authenticity often requires courage because staying aligned with what matters most when the environment around you pushes for compromise can feel uncomfortable.

I hope this fable sparks reflection. And perhaps it will even transform your own leadership journey. So, welcome. The story begins here.

1
Date Night

"HONEY, I'M HOME!" Elena called playfully as she stuck her head around the door into the kitchen, smiling. Oscar's back was to her as he hovered intently over the six-burner Wolf gas range, gracefully maneuvering each pot and pan with ingredients that would eventually become his interpretation of a five-star dinner.

Elena could feel Oscar's radiant smile before he turned to greet her.

"Hello, there! You're earlier than I expected, considering you had to drop the kids off at your parents', run errands, and join your Saturday yoga class," Oscar said.

Oscar's infectious smile glowed ear to ear. Elena walked over and kissed him softly on the lips. He handed her the glass of wine sitting on the center island. "For you. It's your favorite."

Elena sipped the Napa Valley cabernet, relishing the tobacco, chocolate, plum, and blackberry undertones while cycling through memories of their family vacation in Northern California three years ago.

"You know me too well!" she exclaimed.

Oscar smiled and turned his attention back to the stove.

"On tonight's menu, we're having something a little different," he began. "I felt a bit adventurous and wanted to mix things up. For you, my love, as an appetizer, I've prepared a vegan steak tartare using a local mushroom blend and fresh herbs from our garden. The main course is an herb-stuffed whole branzino with roasted rosemary fingerling potatoes and grilled veggies. What do you think?"

"Yes, chef!" she exclaimed before returning to her wine.

"Dinner shall be served in 20 minutes," Oscar replied in a playful, snooty British accent. "Feel free to relax. I'll call you once the table is set."

Wine glass in hand, Elena took the stairs to their bedroom to freshen up. At the suggestion of a couple's therapist, Oscar and Elena had made their weekly date night a tradition several years ago. Married 15 years with the requisite ups and downs, date night was something they both looked forward to. It was a reliable way to integrate their independent but fulfilled selves into their partnership. It was an uninterrupted space where they decompressed, discussed the week's events and experiences, shared hopes for their future, and sometimes connected with friends. They also used the time together to support and encourage one another.

As Elena came back downstairs, Oscar called to her that dinner was ready. She replied by walking into the dining room.

Before serving, Oscar refilled their wine glasses and said, "First, I want to raise a glass to you for showing me so much grace this week. You took care of the kids and gave me enough space to focus on transitioning into my new role. The days were long, and sometimes I wasn't fully present. We didn't even get a chance to talk about the day-to-day. But we made it through. Know that I appreciate you tremendously."

He raised his glass to eye level, and Elena followed suit, the rims clinking as they met in the table's middle.

"So, how was your week?" he continued.

"Honestly, it wasn't very interesting. Oh, but there is some good news. My firm took on a large new corporate client. I'm the assigned partner since the client operates in my sweet spot, the healthcare space. Blah, blah, blah. Other than that, I was lawyering, like I always do," Elena chuckled.

"Oh yeah," she continued, "when the twins get back from my parents' place tomorrow night, I agreed to take them for ice cream to celebrate graduating from fifth grade with honors."

"Uhhh, can I go, too?" Oscar asked.

"Sure, we can make room for you!" Elena grinned. "And how was your big week? First week on the new job as Mr. Chief Operating Officer of Anywhere Banking Corporation. Knowing you, I'm sure you already have some insights and interesting perspectives."

Oscar pondered this for a moment.

Elena broke into his contemplation. "Well?"

"It was an interesting first week. Exciting and interesting," he replied. "My sense is that this will be one of the biggest, if not the largest, challenges of my career."

He took another bite of the succulent branzino before placing his fork on his plate so he could tell her more. His eagerness to finally share his week seemed to pull the words from his mouth.

"ABC has been an incredible company for a long time. But they are in a tough spot and need to find a way out. I spent much of the week meeting with the CEO, my peers on the executive team, my direct reports, and a few key stakeholders. Next week, I'll get a little deeper into the organization."

Elena interjected, "None of that is surprising. You've taken on plenty of new roles, and this sounds like your normal approach. What was interesting about it?"

"Well, you know my longtime mentor Erik was appointed board chair last year. When he reached out to gauge my interest in the COO role, he shared that the company had a few strategic challenges, and he thought the way I infuse authenticity into organizational transformations could be just what ABC needed. Because it's a public company, it's common knowledge that Michael, the CEO, is embattled. The last few years have been very rough on him as the company has lost revenue, increased costs, and struggled with customer service.

"And Michael surprised me this week by informing me that I'm solely responsible for delivering new technology that's designed to improve our customer service capability. The goal is to get our service standards back to best-in-class, which was ABC's position in the market just before Michael became CEO seven years ago," he continued.

"This responsibility makes sense since all operations functions report to me. But Michael seems to be distancing himself a bit, maybe because they have been trying to implement this technology for the past two years and haven't been successful. And, interestingly enough, my last meeting today was with Erik, who shared that Michael did not want to hire me," Oscar explained.

"So, there's already a little tension at the top. Delegating this failed project, and essentially setting up a silo, feels like Michael is giving Erik the proverbial middle finger," Oscar said, wincing.

"Sounds a little intense," Elena said, looking up from her meal.

"There's more," Oscar continued. "My initial perception is the executive team may not be aligned directionally, either. ABC has been around for more than 75 years. Some leaders have spent their entire careers there. Some are relatively new. Strategically, there's a unified desire to build an organization that can thrive in today's environment. But folks seem to be divided on how to do it and what it would look like."

He added butter to his potatoes before continuing.

"I've already identified three or so leadership factions. In my experience, that tends to create political fiefdoms, which can trickle down into an organization. The story I hear from the newer leaders is that not much gets done. Or, if something gets done, it's not to the level desired, yet the leaders celebrate the mediocrity," he observed.

Elena sat back in her seat, looking astonished, "Uhhh, how did you pick up that much information in only the first week?"

Oscar laughed. "I've been at this a long time, babe. You said it yourself. I have my own approach when jumping into new roles. And I listen intently to what people are telling me and what they are not telling me. We are all creatures of habit. Most leaders, despite wanting to do the right thing, default to self-preservation when faced with fear. If the perception is that I'm being brought in against the CEO's will, it will create a few waves," he explained.

"On the other hand, those leaders who want to see change will probably be fully transparent if they see me as credible. And those who don't will tell me what they think I want to hear. Or they'll hold back. I've been doing this long enough to be able to recognize all of it. So, I take notes, and over time, ground any assumptions I develop. That comes through follow-up discussions or conversations with employees who are in the know."

"That's remarkable," Elena said with admiration.

"I appreciate you recognizing one of my many superpowers," Oscar joked. "Listen, I don't want to spend our entire evening talking about my week, but I could really use your insights as I make this transition and get up to speed. Before we head out to meet the crew tonight, do you mind if I tell you a bit more about the players and my early observations?"

"I'll gladly be your ear and offer my perspective where I have one," Elena said.

"I appreciate that," Oscar replied. "Let's start with what ABC is and what we do. Then, I'll go through the key leaders."

He continued, "ABC is one of the largest diversified financial services firms in the U.S. I mentioned earlier that it's been around for about 75 years. Most people know it as a consumer bank that offers credit cards and retail banking services, like checking and savings accounts, personal loans, and the like. But it also has impressive small business, commercial banking, asset management, and investment banking businesses. Over the past ten years, the company has grown predominantly by acquiring smaller competitors — think regional retail banks with large branch footprints, credit card issuers, and smaller brokerage houses. ABC has acquired businesses across its full spectrum of products and services."

Oscar paused to refill their water glasses before continuing.

"As you can imagine, the organization and its structure have consistently evolved. The company has gone through multiple 'transformations' within the past five or six years. None of them seemed to really stick. Plus, there isn't much consistency with how the business units are run, even though our executive team has tried to scale by creating large, centralized teams to support the growing organization.

"A good example is when ABC acquired that credit card company last year. From what I understand, there was a huge fight about what functions should be centralized at an enterprise level. The credit card company CEO prevailed and operates the business as he sees fit, with very little input from the broader ABC. Without integrating functions during the merger, you have a bunch of duplicative costs associated with technology and people. Not to mention, it makes navigating the organization unnecessarily complex.

On top of that, the customer experiences throughout the organization are very different depending on whether a customer is calling about their credit card, retail banking relationship, or investment account. It seems like the complexity, plus the lack of clarity and accountability, are all catching up to ABC," he said.

Elena posed a question, "All that makes sense. What about the leadership team?"

Oscar offered a half smile, "Let's start with Michael, my boss, the CEO. Michael has been the CEO for seven years. He is a really smart guy. MBA from The Wharton School. His entire 35-year career has been spent there, so he knows the company better than anybody. Internally, they call him 'the dealmaker' because of his strong investment banking roots there. He made his mark handling large-scale transactions," he noted.

"About 15 years ago, Michael moved out of investment banking to run ABC's consumer banking arm. Then he ran the international businesses before becoming CEO. From what I understand, he is a relationship guy who values loyalty. I also heard one of the other executives say he can be a bit of a salesman when it comes to new ideas. My sense is that is what's made him so successful in the dealmaking space."

Oscar absent-mindedly folded and unfolded his napkin's corners while continuing.

"Of course, everyone in the C-suite — my peers — reports to him. Lora is the chief technology officer (CTO). She started her career as a programmer and has been with ABC for eight years. Interestingly, HR poached her from a competitor as a potential successor to the then-CTO. It was a smart move — she proved she was worthy and got that role about three years ago. While Lora is technically skilled, she also has an amazingly high EQ plus innate leadership skills. Her vision of technology as a strategic capability is so clear."

Oscar frowned for a moment before telling Elena, "I got the impression from our conversations that she feels she hasn't been given the runway or a seat at the table to push that vision. Instead, her team spends much of its time patching the antiquated technology from all the organizations ABC has acquired over the years."

"It sounds like you respect her already," Elena observed.

"I sense she is very talented but undervalued. Also, she would be a key partner in the strategic change that I'll be responsible for. So yes, it does help to begin to understand and appreciate what she's capable of. I think we'll work well together," Oscar replied.

"Robert is the chief financial officer. He started his career at one of the big accounting firms before joining ABC almost 30 years ago. My understanding is that early on, when ABC was his client, Robert impressed Michael when he audited Michael's business area. Michael recommended him to ABC when there was an opening, and their careers have moved in parallel ever since. When Michael was promoted, he'd find a spot for Robert on his finance team. And that has served both for the past three decades. It's well known that Robert is Michael's right-hand guy."

Elena interjected, "That's not unusual. You see that happen everywhere in business."

"True," Oscar agreed. "And there's nothing wrong with it until it stops serving, creates blinders, or diminishes accountability."

Elena nodded her head while Oscar continued sharing his impressions.

"Phillip, the chief growth officer, is one of the newer executives. He's been at ABC for only four years and, at 39, is the youngest on the executive team. He has a strong understanding of digital capabilities in the financial services space and how they can lead to growth. The CGO role is new to the organization and replaces the chief marketing officer position. Based on my conversations with Phillip, he isn't making enough progress getting leadership buy-in on the growth strategy. I can tell he's frustrated, and he even alluded to looking externally for other opportunities.

"The chief human resources officer is Farouk, who joined ABC seven years ago after leading HR for a large global manufacturing firm. In the manufacturing space, he was well known for his strong focus on people. Unfortunately, it sounds like his voice isn't heard much at the executive table, as he isn't often consulted on the effects of business strategy on people and the ever-evolving culture. He also mentioned that feedback from the last employee opinion survey showed that people are suffering from change fatigue," Oscar said.

"Don't the CEO and other executives care about how people experience all of these transformations?" Elena asked.

"I'm sure they do," Oscar continued. "Sometimes the financial results supersede the people agenda, especially when the organization is trying to stay relevant while protecting the stock price. CFO Robert alluded to how strategic priorities are highly sensitive to the outward-facing market perception. So, their quarter-over-quarter updates really focus on telling a story of their aspirations. Unfortunately, the people agenda gets moved to the back burner. At least that's Farouk's perspective.

"Bijal is the chief risk officer. He has been at ABC for 20 years, five in his current role. Bijal is somewhat conservative, but that perspective really helped ABC weather the financial crisis better than most. He has a solid reputation in the industry for his risk management acumen. *Strong* personality.

"Bijal mentioned he has less and less of an appetite for risk the more ABC tries to transform. He understands that increased complexity raises the organization's risk profile. The words he used to describe the current state are, and I quote, 'ABC is at a tipping point. And we will either come out on the other side, or we will implode.' Let's just say it wasn't the week's most optimistic conversation. I'm interested to see if there is any hyperbole in that statement or if it's the true state of affairs," Oscar said, wrapping up his meet-the-team summary.

"Ouch!" Elena exclaimed.

"I know, right?!" Oscar laughed ruefully. "The way I see it, there is opportunity for me with tremendous upside. Or… I'll go down trying to redirect the ship. But those are the key executives and what I've picked up through conversations. There are a few other folks reporting to the CEO, like presidents of the different business lines. However, the C-suite folks will be the key people I'll interact with as I focus on implementing a strategic change initiative that will improve our customer service capabilities."

Oscar took a few more bites of fish and a quick sip of wine before continuing, "There are two other important leaders on my team I want to tell you about. Darren is the operations head with responsibility for all customer service call centers and back-office functions. He has a very big job with responsibility for more than 40,000 employees — more than 75% of ABC's workforce.

"Before I joined, he reported directly to Michael for a few years. However, he wasn't responsible for all operations. The business unit presidents were responsible for their own product and service lines. This was the result of decision-making similar to when ABC acquired its newest credit card company, and some functions weren't centralized, as I mentioned before. I share that because Darren's role has evolved. During his 25 years at ABC, he has worked in operations leadership positions across multiple product lines. He has developed strong technical knowledge as his career has grown. I know Michael values that because he told me himself. He mentioned he sees Darren as a future successor for my role," he added.

"That's interesting that Michael would call that out for Darren specifically, no?" Elena said.

"Yeah, I thought so, too. It made me wonder whether Michael really wanted Darren for my position," Oscar replied. "I'm sure I'll learn more as I spend additional time with both of them."

Oscar returned to the kitchen to get dessert before continuing.

"The last person to mention is Diana, who also reports to me. She leads the corporate-wide program management and change office. I don't think she's much more than 41 or 42. Diana started at ABC, left for a few years, then returned and has been here for about ten more. She grew up in operations but has led both operations teams and support functions.

"She impressed me during our first one-on-one. Clearly, she aspires to do more. At the same time, she alluded that despite getting more responsibility over the years, she doesn't feel highly valued by the executive team for her thought leadership and other capabilities. She feels like she's been put into a role where she can't be successful because the executive team isn't aligned on change strategy."

Oscar enjoyed a spoonful of tiramisu from the family's favorite bakery before continuing.

"Diana described her role as a task master for changes happening in the organization. More importantly, she says she often finds out about changes only after they've failed, and people call her team to help fix the problems that result. Darren is her largest internal 'customer.' I sensed Diana may get frustrated with that relationship because Darren is the elder statesman on my leadership team. Oh, and I almost forgot! The executive team selected Diana to lead the strategic change initiative, and since that hasn't gone well, there is a need for damage control. So, we'll be working together closely.

"Alright, that's it. I appreciate you letting me share a little about the players at ABC. It feels good to have a space to unload a bit. Thank you!"

Oscar leaned over and gave Elena a peck on the cheek. "If you're finished with your dessert, I'll clear the table and clean up the kitchen. Then we can get ready to head out."

After finishing her wine and handing her husband the glass, Elena observed, "I'm not sure how much help I was, but it was my pleasure to just sit and listen. I know it's early, but what's next?"

Oscar rose from the table and began loading the dishwasher while he replied, "First, I need to spend more time with Diana to discuss the change initiative and where she is with everything. And I've made a few presumptions about the organization and its leaders that I need to confirm. That process will lead to questions and ideas. Things will get clearer over time. And once I'm confident I understand the full context, I'll develop a strategy and do my best to deliver on that.

"None of that is new," he continued, "but the context really does matter. My last few positions were in private companies that didn't have to play to market expectations in the same way that public companies do. I've repeatedly seen where short-term and long-term goals conflict. In private companies, I've been able to perform well in part because there is less complexity to navigate. Regardless, I'll bring all of me to this organization and do my best. We will see how everyone responds to that."

Oscar flashed a quick smile. "I'm optimistic. On a lighter note, what did you think of my branzino?" They both laughed. He finished cleaning up the kitchen before they changed their clothes and headed out for drinks and dancing with friends.

As he locked the front door, though, Oscar couldn't help but say a silent prayer that his brand of authenticity-infused change management would be enough to turn things around at ABC.

2
Context Matters

MONDAY CAME QUICKLY, and for Oscar, work started early. By 8:30, he had already drunk two cups of coffee while getting caught up on emails and reviewing five business performance presentations. His executive assistant, Shannon, had printed his materials for the day's meetings and placed them neatly on the left corner of his desk. He was about to review them when he was interrupted by a soft knock on the large, open glass door.

Focus broken, Oscar looked up to see Shannon in the doorway.

"Hi, Oscar. Are you ready for Diana now?"

"Thanks, Shannon," Oscar replied. "Yes, please send her in."

Shannon waved Diana over and showed her to the cozy sitting area in Oscar's office. Before taking a seat on one of the matching rustic leather accent chairs, Diana discreetly observed how Oscar had arranged his office. He was at his desk at one end, facing the group seating in the middle. At the far end was a small conference table with chairs. Each section took up a third of the spacious office.

Oscar rose from his desk and joined Diana, sitting on the loveseat directly across from her.

"Good morning, Diana. It's good to see you again. How was your weekend?" Oscar asked.

"It was good, I guess. I didn't do anything special. How

about you?" Diana replied apprehensively.

"Mine was pretty good. It was a chance to recover from my first week of drinking from the firehose. I guess I'd better get used to that," he joked. "My wife and I spent some time with friends and took our twins out for ice cream to celebrate their graduation from the fifth grade."

"Oh, all that sounds like fun," Diana replied politely.

Sensing Diana's unease, Oscar quickly shifted to the reason for their meeting. "I appreciate you taking the time to meet with me so early. Personally, I'm not much of a morning person. But I wanted to make sure to touch base with you early this week to discuss the strategic change initiative, Project One."

Oscar could hear Diana's hard gulp. Her discomfort was palpable as she repositioned her tense body in the chair. Diana felt her face flush as her blood pressure went up.

"Are you okay?" Oscar asked.

"Yes, I'm fine," Diana swiftly replied.

"Are you sure? Maybe I'm misreading the signals here, but I sense some tension. What's wrong? It's okay. There's nothing you can say that is off limits," Oscar said reassuringly.

Diana let out a large exhale. "Well, can I just ask? Are you firing me?"

Taken aback, Oscar's eyes widened as he reflexively leaned back on the sofa. "Of course not!" he said, his surprise obvious. "Why would you think that?"

Diana let out a large sigh before responding.

"We always let people go on Monday mornings or Friday afternoons. And I know there has been a lot of noise about how we haven't delivered on Project One, which is my responsibility. I've seen people who don't have strong relationships at the top here get fired quickly if something goes wrong," she began.

"And since you've said nothing's off limits, I'll add that I've noticed that those who have relationships in high places tend to be rewarded for what I consider to be mediocre outcomes, or their bad performances are swept under the rug. I'm not the only one who thinks that, either. We all know that new leaders often bring in their own teams, too. So, I can't help but feel like my head is on the chopping block," she said, surprising even herself with how she unloaded everything she had been thinking all weekend.

Knowing how important his body language was at this pivotal moment, Oscar leaned towards her to explain. "Let me be clear. This isn't a conversation about you losing your job. Whenever I join a new organization, I spend the first 90 days understanding context. I try to learn how the people and the systems they've built operate. That comes through observation and talking to people.

"I know Project One has been challenging, and there is a lot of pressure from Michael and the board to deliver value," he continued. "We will get there. But I wanted to start diving in quickly since we don't have time on our side. And I don't generally make changes without getting background first and understanding why we are where we are. I like to draw my own conclusions rather than operate from someone else's agenda.

"If it's any consolation, our introductory conversation from last week gave me the strong impression that you are very capable. Understanding what went wrong with Project One and how we want to course correct is where I was hoping we could spend our energy this morning," he concluded.

Surprised, Diana responded, "Oh! That's a relief! I appreciate that you shared that."

Oscar could see that his explanation created a shift in Diana's demeanor, but he needed to think about how to continue building her trust.

"Let me be transparent and maybe even a little vulnerable with you for a second," Oscar said.

"Yes, new leaders often come into roles with a new perspective as they see opportunities for change. And that may lead to some level of leadership turnover. However, it's premature for me to make those decisions right now. In this very moment, you hold a lot of power. I need you as much as you need me because you have all the history and insight about what's working and not working well here. And for the sake of this conversation, you're also the expert on Project One.

"I will talk to other key stakeholders about that effort, but I really am beholden to your input about what went wrong and how we may want to move forward. From that vantage point, you and I will work together to figure out our future approach. We will both play the roles of teacher and student for one another. Make sense?"

Diana nodded, visibly relieved, and picked up her pad and pen to take notes.

Oscar continued, "So, let's start with the basics, shall we? I know the initiative's high-level focus is to leverage a proprietary artificial intelligence-based technology to integrate each customer service center into one centralized operation. The AI is so advanced that customer service advisors won't have to know every product and service detail. That means we could create a one-stop shop type of customer service organization. Is that a good characterization?"

"Yes, at a high level, that is exactly what we want to do," Diana responded.

"What are some of the benefits we'll get from this?" Oscar asked.

Diana confidently replied, "There are financial, risk, and customer experience benefits. From a cost perspective, we would need fewer advisors taking calls. In addition, our total ownership cost for the existing technology platforms would decrease as we combine data storage, sunset old legacy systems, and roll out a new and highly intuitive user platform. Net-net, the total cost reduction is pretty significant and helps us achieve profit margins aligned with the market's expectations over the next three to five years."

"Talk to me about how this will improve our customer service," Oscar prompted.

"Well, implementing new automated workflows also allows us to eliminate processes that have historically failed without some type of manual intervention. Over the years, those manual processes have led to significant financial losses and customer escalations. So, we would be reducing our financial, operational, and reputational risks. We expect this to be a vast improvement in our overall ability to satisfactorily handle calls coming into all business unit customer service operations. And since none of our competitors have technology this advanced, we believe it will create a competitive advantage," Diana said.

"Excellent!" Oscar exclaimed. "The business case sounds very well-thought-out. This is exciting! Is the rest of the organization fired up about this?"

Diana hesitated. "I'd say it's a mixed bag."

Oscar grabbed a pen and pad from his desk and returned to the couch. "Tell me more," he urged.

"The executive team doesn't seem to be on the same page about why this is important and how we should deliver the solutions," Diana began. "Let me quickly walk through what I'm seeing from each person on the leadership team."

She started at the top. "Michael has been clear that there is pressure from the board to make this happen. Robert, the CFO, has been focused on cost implications and generally sides with Michael. Lora, our CTO, believes this is the right thing to do, but she sees a bigger strategic possibility that goes beyond the original business case and Michael's desire to save face with the board and the market.

"There are additional use cases like email messages and website chat where our AI solution could create benefits and further support our resulting market differentiation. I think Phillip — he's the chief growth officer — is stuck on the lack of focus on real growth. So, his support comes and goes. Our HR head, Farouk, is concerned about how we deliver the change and whether our employees have the appetite for such a large disruption. Interestingly, as the chief risk officer, Bijal thinks we are adding too much complexity.

"And then there's Darren, who, of course, you know better than the others probably because he's operations head. He prefers to keep all the operational functions separate, almost in silos. Privately, he believes it's just easier for him and his team to manage things the way they are now. But he won't go against what Michael says is the direction," she notes, wrapping up.

"Interesting," Oscar pondered aloud. "Honestly, none of that is surprising. During my first week, I could tell there wasn't clear alignment on the organization's priorities. So, it's not shocking to think our leaders aren't unified on Project One. This is common in many organizations, more so in those that are distressed or under intense pressure. Have you thought about how we need to pivot?"

"I have," Diana replied reluctantly. "But I don't have a clear path forward. We generally don't manage change very well here, despite being well-intended. Historically, new initiatives limp along for a stretch. Maybe someone gets fired for not delivering. More likely than not, the initiative will quietly die. Suddenly, no one is talking about it anymore. Then we restructure. I don't feel like we have ever really 'transformed' the business in any meaningful way."

Oscar stood up from the couch and walked to the whiteboard near his desk.

"Do you mind if I share a framework that has worked well for me in the past?" he asked.

"Please do," Diana replied.

Oscar continued. "I've done a lot of transformation work throughout my career. In fact, I only accept opportunities where I can come in and build something new — that's what attracted me to ABC. I get my energy from leading transformations. It's where I feel I create the most value.

"Now, if you talk to any of the people I've worked with or led in the past, they will probably tell you that I am highly authentic. What I've learned through experience, research, and mentors is that authenticity can be leveraged as a capability to elevate people and organizations."

Diana interrupted. "I'm not sure I follow."

Oscar continued. "When you think of authenticity for yourself, what does that mean to you? How do you show up? How do you feel?"

Diana thought for a moment before responding, "I feel like I can be my true self."

"Okay, and how do you feel when you are your true self?" Oscar asked.

Diana began to perk up, "I feel free, sometimes even excited. There are fewer limitations."

"Exactly!" Oscar exclaimed. "Notice how by even just thinking about it, your energy has shifted. I could see and feel the difference when you responded."

"But what does that have to do with transformation and Project One?" Diana probed.

"Before I answer that, let me offer some definitions that create a foundation for authenticity," Oscar continued as he grabbed a dry-erase marker and faced the whiteboard.

"I want to share three types of authenticity. I call the first individual authenticity. Think about this as authenticity in humans. It's the relationship between our internal thoughts, values, and beliefs and our subsequent actions and behaviors. Note that one is intrinsic, and one is extrinsic. The more aligned those intrinsic and extrinsic aspects feel, the more authentic we are. The less aligned those aspects are, the less authentic we feel," he said.

"I think that makes sense," Diana replied. "If I'm in a meeting and I feel like I can speak up and share my thoughts, that is an example of me feeling more authentic. On the other hand, if it doesn't feel safe to speak up for whatever reason, I feel less authentic. Is that right?"

Oscar smiled broadly, saying, "That's exactly right, Diana! And note how those higher and lower authenticity experiences feel in your body. When we feel highly authentic, there's a sense of what I call resonance or alignment. When we feel less authentic, we feel resistant because we sense we lack alignment, even if we can't label it that way. Those are two important aspects that I'll come back to."

FIGURE 1. INDIVIDUAL AUTHENTICITY

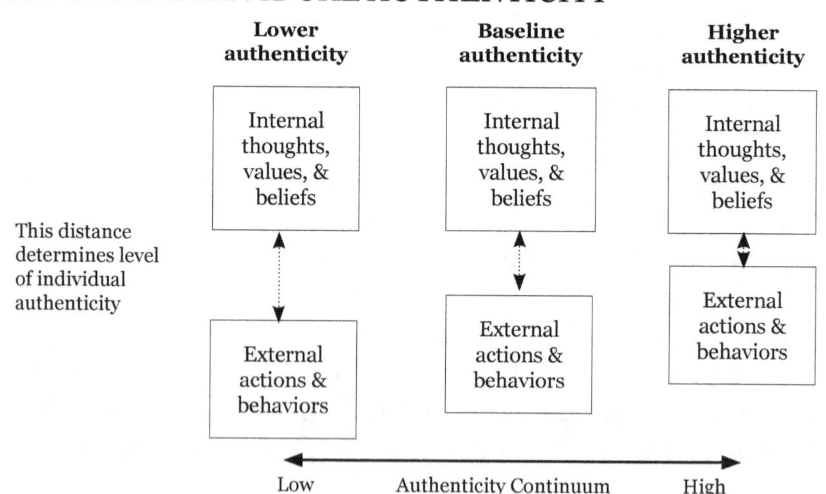

Oscar continued with his explanation. "Because those intrinsic and extrinsic aspects are always present, we are always authentic. It's just a matter of to what degree. And our authenticity level changes as we navigate different experiences and contexts. That leads me to the second type of authenticity, collective authenticity.

"Every group has its own authenticity. Let's take ABC for example. The organization has shared thoughts, values, and beliefs. And from those aspects come expected actions and behaviors. We might call this culture. And again, there is a relationship between these intrinsic and extrinsic aspects that we observe and experience on a group level.

"Do group members operate at a high level of resonance with one another? If so, the group is experiencing higher authenticity. And vice versa. Just think about the resistance you may feel when at work and how much energy is spent simply managing the resistance for yourself or others," he noted.

Diana nodded.

"The relationship between individual and collective authenticity is where things get more interesting and potentially complex," Oscar continued. "With individual authenticity, only the individual can determine their personal authenticity level. That's influenced by their past experiences along with their thoughts, values, and beliefs. Nobody else has access to what makes that individual feel authentic.

"With collective authenticity, we are dealing with expected actions and behaviors for group members. This is about individual conformity to the collective norm. So, whether or not you're conforming to what's expected — what makes the group authentic — is determined not by you but by someone else. That's usually a group member. They base that conclusion on what they observe about how you're acting according to what's expected," he continued.

"When you combine individual and collective authenticity, as in our case with an employee working for an organization, there is a natural tension because who the employee wants to be and who they are expected to be are often in conflict. That can create resistance for both the employee and the organization."

Oscar paused. "Let's take a moment. Does all of that make sense so far?"

FIGURE 2. COLLECTIVE AUTHENTICITY

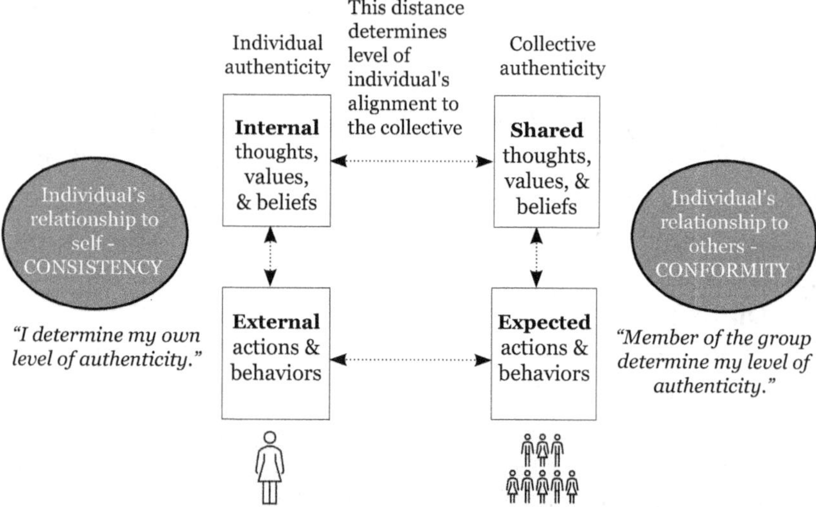

"Yes, I think it does," Diana said pensively. "Do you mind if I share an example for clarification for your feedback?"

"Go ahead," Oscar said.

"ABC has been around for 75 years. The culture has acquired a clear, but unstated, dress code. Executives generally follow a professional dress code, while everyone else follows business casual. That means that wearing khakis to a meeting with an executive would go against cultural norms. Someone who isn't aware of the unspoken dress code might feel uneasy or embarrassed if someone pointed out they made a wardrobe mistake. Plus, their peers might judge them. All that, combined with the fact that the employee doesn't feel like themself in anything but khakis at work, has the potential to create tension, right?" Diana asked.

"Yes! That's a good example," Oscar replied. "To take it a step further, think about people who might be the first in their families to work in a corporate environment, or who haven't been exposed to corporate norms. They risk feeling out of place or being judged for how they show up. So, it's important to understand why this tension may exist. Now, let's take this one step further before we connect to our transformation work and Project One," he said.

"I call the third type of authenticity manifested authenticity. This describes the individuals' and the group's collective output. Products and services have their own authenticity level that reflects the employees and organizations that produce them.

"Let's consider a consumer electronics company that produces a tablet. Customers applaud the product's beautiful design and ease of use. Keep in mind that its design and technical specifications reflect the employees and the organization. That means if the organization has a world-class design team that leaves the company, the product's design will inevitably change over time. The new team will create and interact differently from its predecessor. Those differences can't help but lead to a different product outcome," Oscar explained.

FIGURE 3. MANIFESTED AUTHENTICITY

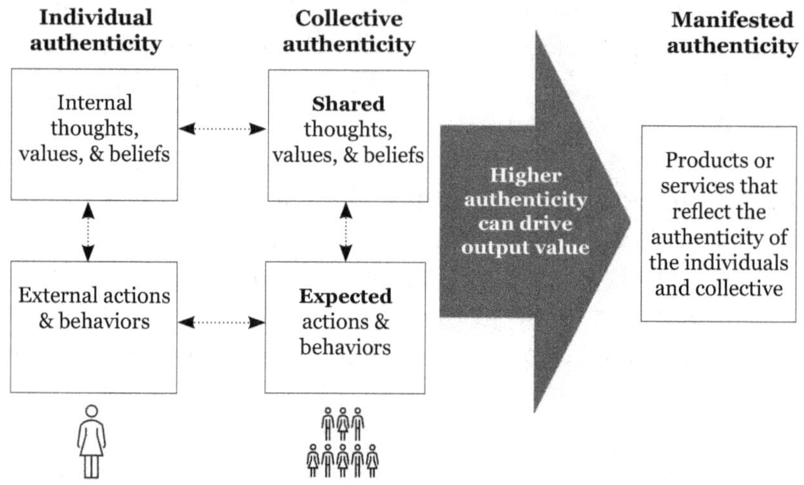

"Now let's apply this information to transformation at ABC. I've seen how highly authentic leaders can reshape an organization's culture. They are transparent and vulnerable, and their behavior aligns with what they think and believe. This is an attractive state in any environment, and in the workplace, followers tend to emulate those leaders. That, in turn, creates environments with trust, psychological safety, optimism, and a host of other positive outcomes.

"The key is that perspectives can change when high authenticity is in the air. And, based on that change in perspective, new outcomes are created. Think about it. ABC creates a certain customer service outcome that reflects the individual employees' and the collective organization's current authenticity. To create a different outcome — to transform, if you will — changing employee and organizational authenticity will eventually produce a different outcome."

Oscar paused to take a sip from his water bottle. "Going back to my original question about how it feels when you are more authentic, and knowing the outcome reflects the employees and organization, do you think our employees would have a better experience designing and delivering new outcomes if they resonate with themselves and the organization, or if they feel resistant?"

"That's easy," Diana replied. "If what's happening resonates with them personally, I imagine they feel they can show up as they are. They will feel heard. And they would feel they are a part of something bigger than themselves. When I think about my own experiences with higher authenticity, everything just felt easier, which means it took less energy."

"Yes," Oscar confirmed. "And all that will be reflected in employee outcomes, even though they're not always something tangible, something you can see. When I think about change management, it's not about introducing or executing a new set of strategies or processes. It's about shifting perspectives. Here, most of our heavy lifting will be spent getting our organizational stakeholders to move from resistance to resonance. The change will not happen if we don't create enough energetic momentum that resonates with the desired outcome. Everything else falls in line after that," Oscar said.

"I'm sure that is not as easy as it sounds. But it makes sense," Diana said thoughtfully.

"Good. I'm glad this is sticking," Oscar replied. "By the way, one last insight. Fear diminishes authenticity more than anything else. If you want to get people resisting, threaten their job or sense of well-being with punishment if they don't perform properly. That's important to remember," he added.

"Wow!" he exclaimed. "Time has really flown by! I have a 9:00 call I don't want to be late for. Do you have any free time after 4 today?"

"I do," Diana replied, smiling.

"Let's reconnect then. I'd like to pick this conversation back up and talk about change phases and how they connect to authenticity. I think it will help us block and tackle our change process as we relaunch Project One. Between now and this afternoon, I'd like you to think about the overall project team structure. Let's spend some time discussing that. I have an executive team meeting on Friday and would like to outline our pivot for the relaunch and begin engaging the key stakeholders. Sound good?"

Feverishly taking notes, Diana replied without looking up, "Yep. Perfect."

"Great. I'll see you at 4," Oscar said.

As Diana exited the office, he added something to the whiteboard.

FIGURE 4. PHASES OF CHANGE

Diana smiled all the way to her next meeting. She was thrilled not to be fired, but she was also excited about her new boss's willingness to share insights into change management. For the first time in a long time, she felt seen and heard by someone on the executive team.

Meanwhile, Oscar was equally pleased with the meeting's outcome. Despite the large project at hand, he felt optimistic that Diana's openness and willingness to experience a new perspective on change would yield positive benefits for Project One and ABC. Oscar took a moment to acknowledge his first small win before launching Microsoft Teams for his 9:00 call.

3

The Framework

DIANA RETURNED TO Oscar's office at 4 p.m., her enthusiasm almost visible in her energy. Shannon wasn't in her cubicle outside the office, so Diana knocked softly on the door, which was slightly ajar.

Oscar looked up. "Come in and have a seat," he said.

"Hi, Oscar," Diana said with a smile as she returned to the sitting area they had used that morning.

Oscar smiled back and walked towards the whiteboard. "I hope you had some time to think about our chat this morning. There's a lot I want us to try and cover over the next hour. As you were leaving before, I added a few more notes to the whiteboard. Let's continue talking about authenticity and change management and discuss the future structure for Project One. Sound good?"

Diana nodded.

"Great," Oscar continued. "I know there are a lot of different change management approaches out there. In my mind, change is about shifting perspectives rather than completing activities. I like to think of change as happening in three phases. The phases are awareness, acceptance, and assimilation. Let's discuss them and see how we can integrate both of our perspectives into a new approach for Project One.

"Let's start with awareness. As context, I'd argue that highly authentic people are also highly self-aware. Yes, we all have parts of ourselves that we aren't fully conscious of. However, to 'know thyself' requires 'higher awareness of thyself.' People can't knowingly change what they aren't aware of. So, moving people from unawareness to awareness at the start is key. On a fundamental level, people need to be aware of the change and what it means to them," he said.

"That makes sense," Diana agreed.

"When you think about driving awareness, what tools or templates do we use in our current change process that might support this phase?" Oscar asked.

"Well, we start with a business case that's reviewed with senior leaders," Diana began. "After it's approved, we develop a change roadmap, identify stakeholders, and even perform road shows to share the planned change more broadly. But like I mentioned previously, we rarely follow that process. My teams often get brought in when something has gone wrong, and we find ourselves muddling through confusion."

"I see," Oscar replied. "Don't be discouraged. It's not unusual for organizations to lack change management discipline. For the sake of integrating our perspectives, let's place the tools and activities you just mentioned under awareness on the board."

He grabbed the black dry-erase marker and began writing before continuing.

"I call the second phase acceptance. And this is where we start to introduce some complexity. Acceptance and agreement together are a beautiful thing. But true acceptance is about coming to terms with reality — your own and others. From a change perspective, it's about acknowledging the way things are and/or the way things will be. During a change, stakeholders may experience many emotions. When they're in an emotional state, it can be difficult to see things as they truly are," Oscar said.

"And, while some stakeholders feel like they're gaining something, others may feel the opposite, like they're losing something. Acceptance means we acknowledge those truths and are still willing to move forward. This is the most difficult change phase. Can you think of any tools or activities that might support this phase?" he asked.

Diana hesitated for a moment before saying, "What about risk assessments or readiness plans?"

"Exactly!" Oscar exclaimed, clearly pleased. "Establishing metrics, success criteria, and so on is part of this phase. Acceptance is where the rubber meets the road to ensure alignment."

Oscar paused to sip from his water bottle.

"Let's move on to the final phase, assimilation. This one is all about blending perspectives as individuals and the environment change. The assimilation process ends when the organization achieves the desired outcome. Stakeholders are behaving differently, meeting success measures, and creating new outcomes. What tools and activities would you include in this phase?"

"I'd imagine training, implementation plans, and the actual execution or launch," Diana replied.

Oscar nodded before saying, "Yes, I agree. We'd also want to include items like post-launch metrics and measurements and post-implementation communication plans because all will support our end goal. Give me a moment, and I'll write a few more examples that I think fit under each phase. You fill in anything you think I might've missed," Oscar said, turning back to the board.

Diana stood up as she watched him quickly add bullets beneath each phase. She could almost feel the stream of consciousness flowing through his hands to the whiteboard.

After a few minutes, Oscar paused and took a step back, scanning for completeness. "How does that look?" he asked.

Diana studied it carefully, then picked up another marker and began making her own additions. After a few minutes, she stepped back before saying, "I think this is complete!"

They reviewed the list together before smiling at each other in full acknowledgement and appreciation of what they had just co-created.

FIGURE 5. CHANGE MANAGEMENT PROCESS FRAMEWORK

Awareness	Acceptance	Acceptance	Assimilation	Assimilation	Assimilation
• Business case	• Current & future state process mapping	• Training strategy	• Training success / readiness measures	• Gate reviews	• Benefits realization measures / metrics
• Change roadmap	• Alignment measure	• Ongoing change updates	• Training evaluation / assessment	• Go / no go recommendation	• Initial implementation retrospective
• Roadshows	• Risk assessment	• Change champion program	• Early exposure opportunities (user testing, sprint reviews, road shows, etc. – build into change & comms plans)	• Implementation support model	• Steady state readiness plans
• Stakeholder inventory	• Compliance & control plans	• Readiness execution plans		• Steady state acceptance criteria	• Close out - after action / retrospective
• Initial change & comms plan	• Readiness plans	• Readiness metrics / dashboards			
• Governance model	• Gate review process / plan	• Confidence checks	• Implementation orchestration plan		
✓ Decision model	• Pulse surveys	• Roadshows			
✓ Team agreements	• Leadership forums, newsletters, etc.				
✓ Decision log	• Change mgmt. training for leaders then staff				
• Current & future state process mapping					

"I like this idea of integrating our perspectives," Diana said, sounding almost surprised.

"Well, if we both contribute to the solution, we both feel aligned with the outcome and have a sense of ownership for it," Oscar replied. "Most importantly, though, we both know we've been seen and heard."

Diana pondered for a moment, "Is this about authenticity?"

"It sure is," Oscar grinned. "In a very simple way, we have just created alignment between our individual authenticity and the collective authenticity that exists when we collaborate. And we've demonstrated transparency and collaboration that increase our psychological safety and trust."

"Ahhh! Totally makes sense!" Diana exclaimed.

"I'm glad this is all coming together," Oscar said. "Next, did you get a chance to think about the project team structure?"

Flipping through her notebook, Diana replied, "I did. Here is what I came up with so far. There isn't much change in key project team members. We need representation from customer service operations, finance, risk management, technology, marketing, human resources, and the project management office. During the last project attempt, core team members were direct reports to C-suite leaders. There were also some other departmental representatives and subject matter experts who were deeper in the organization."

"That makes sense," Oscar replied. "And I imagine the areas that had the most participants were probably coming from Darren's operations teams?"

"Yes. Darren had representation from all his operations areas. There were probably 100 representatives from his teams alone," Diana answered.

"Wow! That seems like a lot," Oscar exclaimed.

"It was a bit overwhelming," Diana admitted. "Keep in mind we intended to transition all operations to one platform, though."

"So, the approach was a big bang where everyone transitioned at once?" Oscar inquired.

"Yes," Diana replied.

"Ouch! That would be extremely difficult for anyone to deliver, especially with new technology," Oscar observed.

"I agree, but there was so much pressure to get this done as quickly as possible that we didn't feel like we had much choice," Diana replied.

Oscar sighed. "I see. One question for you, then. Who was responsible for making decisions about the project, like whether we were ready to implement changes or not?"

"The project team made all decisions, and we'd share them with Darren. He would then report the results up to the executive team," Diana relayed.

Oscar dove deeper. "So, the very large project team came to a consensus, that consensus was shared with Darren, and Darren updated the executive team on the initiative's progress? And all stakeholders involved with the project had equal say in whether changes were implemented or not?"

Hesitantly, Diana replied, "Yes, that's correct."

"Got it," Oscar said. "Let me share my initial impressions. One, I like how you're thinking about the working project team. I think you have the right stakeholder levels there. But it sounds like the project team operated independently from other key stakeholders, like the executive team. In addition, there was no leadership around decision-making, since everyone involved had an equal say. Does that sound accurate?"

"Mmm hmm," Diana replied.

"I'd like to suggest a few modifications," Oscar continued. "First, I believe we'd benefit from a steering committee. This would be a portion of the executive team that ensures the project team gets what they need, helps with escalations, and ensures alignment with top leaders. If you think about who has accountability at the executive level, it would be Lora, whose team is delivering the technology, and me. So, it's critical that we're both aligned on this. Every other steering committee member may provide input or advice, but she and I need to be in lockstep to ensure project team members are moving in unison.

"Second, from a decision-making perspective, since I am ultimately responsible for running operations, I will be the decision-maker for go/no-go decisions. Darren will be my delegate and decision-maker for other project-related decisions. But our readiness to go live will be on me. And that decision will be based on advice and guidance from key stakeholders on the project team. I want to hear any concerns or risks that may be on their minds," he outlined.

"Normally, I'd push decision-making down into the organization. However, this approach is new. We need more operational maturity with it before I can turn that over. So, I'll model the behaviors we want for the future with the expectation that other leaders will adopt them. In time, we can change the decision-maker based on project performance," he said before drinking from his water bottle again.

"Lastly, I suggest we move away from a big bang approach and instead start by selecting one business unit's customer service operation to migrate to the new technology platform. This is a very complex implementation. Each unit has its own intricacies that we need to address and account for. We also need to prove it works before we engage the broader enterprise.

"A successful pilot implementation is a big win and can help create momentum for future phases. This will also allow you to reduce the number of project stakeholders from Darren's area by getting laser-focused on specific products and use cases. My suggestion is we start with the least complex operations. Any idea what business unit that is?"

"I'm pretty sure it's the credit card group, but I can confirm that with Darren," Diana replied.

"Yes, please do that so the three of us are on the same page," Oscar said. "So, what do you think of these changes?"

"They all make sense to me," Diana responded, taking a brief pause from capturing Oscar's guidance in her notebook. "When we do our kickoff, I'll share the strategic changes we're putting in place to help the team grasp what we're changing and why."

"That would be wise," Oscar said. "You focus on maintaining alignment within the project team. I'll do the same with the steering committee and executive team. Our agreement on this will help you and me work through any issues that come up during the project. And they will come up, so let's be prepared," he warned.

"For next steps, can you turn these framework details we've just mapped out here into a presentation slide deck and summarize the project pivots and team structure for the Project One relaunch and have it to me by noon on Wednesday? I'd like to share a preview with Michael in our one-on-one on Thursday. I'd also like to be prepared to provide an update at the executive team meeting Friday morning. Once the execs agree with what we've got here, you can repurpose the slides for discussion with the project team," he concluded.

Diana replied, "Sure, that's no problem. I like the plan."

"Excellent! I look forward to us getting started. I think that's all for now, but let me know if you need anything between now and Wednesday. Have a great night!" Oscar said as he put the markers back.

Diana tucked her notebook into her bag and walked back to her office. There, she immediately began documenting her notes into PowerPoint slides. Even though most around her were leaving, Diana spent the next hour following Oscar's instructions. Despite the longer than expected workday, she felt energized. She was hopeful and optimistic about Oscar's plan, believing it would help create the outcomes she was responsible for delivering more than two years ago.

Later that week, Oscar met with Michael as scheduled to share his plan for moving forward with Project One. In Oscar's mind, the pivot was rational and made sense, so he was pleased that Michael agreed and encouraged him to share the proposed changes with the executive team the next day.

On Friday morning, Oscar spent 20 minutes discussing the changes with the group. He recommended a cross-functional steering committee that included himself, Lora, Bijal, Robert, and Farouk. He noted that it would help them incorporate each function's perspectives so they could create the best outcome for the organization. Each executive agreed to participate.

The week closed with Oscar updating Erik, the board chair, on the new Project One plan. Erik was impressed that Oscar had made so much progress already and requested ongoing updates because the initiative was so important to the corporation's success.

For the next two weeks, Oscar and Diana worked closely to communicate the relaunch plan to key stakeholders and the organization overall. There was some skepticism, but more often than not, people were enthusiastic and optimistic.

The team began executing the plan, but it wasn't long before Oscar and Diana began running into challenges. Oscar could see how old leadership behaviors threatened their ability to implement the changes he knew were necessary to move ABC forward. Despite getting buy-in from the executive team and key stakeholders upfront, Oscar saw that completing Project One wouldn't be quite as simple or easy as letting the new guy run with a new plan. He and Diana had their work cut out for them.

4
Resistance and Resonance

ABOUT FOUR WEEKS into the Project One relaunch, Diana requested a one-on-one with Oscar to discuss project team challenges and her overall concern that the project wasn't getting the traction needed to deliver as promised.

They scheduled the meeting for the next afternoon. Coincidentally, Oscar spotted Diana staring out the three-story glass windows in the main lobby as he headed back to his office for their meeting. As he approached from the side, Diana, her eyes still fixed on the horizon, asked, "Do you ever wonder how such a big organization with so much incredible history continues to exist even when there are such long periods of infighting, dysfunction, and chaos?"

"Wow, that's a grim way to begin our meeting," Oscar said, smiling in spite of Diana's tone.

She half-smiled as she turned toward him before continuing. "I've just been thinking about this uphill battle with Project One. It feels like today's challenges are the culmination of a lot of different things, past and present. Some people want a different future, while others want things to remain the same. Good and talented people leave to pursue new opportunities while others, preferring the status quo, stay, and we start the cycle all over again."

"I know exactly what you mean. Where is all this coming from, though?" Oscar asked.

Before responding, Diana turned away again so he

wouldn't see that she was becoming upset. "Today, one of my closest friends here, Lisa, announced she's leaving for a competitor. Lisa is the division head of the credit card customer service operations. She grew up here and has so much subject matter expertise and institutional knowledge. I will really miss working with her, but I also want her to be happy and fulfilled, so it bothers me that it can't happen here. I also think it will be impossible to replace her on the project team," Diana explained, her voice sounding as sad as she felt.

Oscar remembered meeting Lisa and being impressed with her leadership, transparency, and business knowledge in general. He knew that other executive team members also thought highly of her. This felt like a potentially big loss for both Project One and the organization.

Oscar knew he needed to break the mood quickly, so he said, "You know what? It's such a beautiful afternoon. Let's walk and talk instead of meeting in my office like we usually do. I know a spot a few blocks from here where we can chat, and walking there will be good for us. Are you up for that?"

"Sure," Diana replied, a little surprised.

Hoping to shift the mood, Oscar smiled broadly as he held the door open for her. The duo walked silently for several minutes before turning into an alley with a small, stand-alone brick building with a cheery, bright yellow door and a matching yellow-framed picture window. The small sign above the door read, "Patisserie et Mes Amies"; the hand-lettered chalkboard leaning against the building teased passersby with the day's fresh-from-the-oven specials.

Oscar ushered Diana in just before the three people behind the counter all called out in unison, "Ossccaarr!"

Confused by the celebrity greeting, Diana turned to him for an explanation.

Oscar matched the greeting's energy. "Hey! How are you all? Long time, no see!"

A dark-haired gentleman wearing a white, double-breasted chef's jacket stepped forward, smiling at the pair. "Well, it has been a full week, Oscar," he said with a French accent. "And who did you bring with you?" He extended his hand to greet Diana.

"My name is Diana. Oscar is my manager," Diana replied, smiling.

Oscar, who never liked the idea of someone working for him, gently corrected her. "Diana and I work together, Andre. She is a very talented leader at ABC, and I thought today was a great day to introduce her to this hidden gem."

"Well, welcome, welcome, Diana!" Andre exclaimed. "I hope you will enjoy our little patisserie. What can we get the two of you?"

Diana studied the dozen or so pastries neatly displayed behind the glass case. Meanwhile, Oscar requested his regular, an almond croissant and coffee.

"There are so many interesting choices! What would you recommend?" Diana asked.

"They are all delicious, of course! But if I had to steer you towards something for your first experience, I'd recommend the fresh blueberry financier," the pastry chef suggested.

"Financier? How relevant," Diana laughed.

"Oh, I get it. Financier! ABC!" Andre laughed. "In this case, a financier is an almond-based cake that is light and moist in the middle but has a wonderful little crisp crust on the outside. These are freshly baked, and we just got the blueberries this morning from a local farm, so everything's as fresh as can be," he said with obvious pride.

"I'll take one, then, and a coffee," Diana replied with a smile.

"Magnifique! Your orders are coming right up," Andre

exclaimed as Oscar paid the cashier. "Monsieur Oscar, you can see that your favorite table by the window is available. We'll bring your pastries and coffees over momentarily. Make yourselves comfortable."

Oscar didn't waste time with small talk while they waited for their orders. "Can we go back to the discussion about Lisa?" he asked as soon as they sat down. "It seems like her planned departure really upsets you. Any idea why she is leaving?"

"Lisa has been at ABC for more than 20 years. She is convinced that now, more than ever, Project One will never get over the line. Her team's participation in the project for the past two years was very taxing, and she doesn't want to go through that again."

"And why does she believe Project One won't be successful?" Oscar asked.

"Can I share something with you in confidence?" Diana requested.

Oscar nodded as he sipped his coffee, delivered with the pastries just moments before.

"There are two things at play. First, ABC tends to run in cycles. The company wants to transform. So, we bring in new leaders who have the experience to help us. But the old guard tends to not really change. Lisa described it as being on a hamster wheel of change. She's just tired of it.

"Second, Lisa and Darren aren't on the same page. She is a Project One advocate because she understands the benefits for our customers, her teams, and the organization. But Darren has made it clear to his direct reports that he doesn't support combining the customer service operations across the enterprise. Also, Lisa shared with me that during our first attempt at Project One, Darren's opinionated updates to the executive team caused some to believe the business case wasn't strong enough. That eventually led to us stopping the work."

"Darren isn't on the same page?" Oscar asked, clearly surprised. "Really? We have talked extensively about it, and he has offered his team's full support."

"Yeah, key here is 'his team's full support,'" Diana explained. "All his direct reports leading the business-unit-level customer service operations are on board. But the buck seems to stop with Darren. Since the executive team only hears his voice, his perspective is the only one that seems to matter. Our CEO, Michael, thinks highly of Darren and trusts his judgment. Lisa thinks that makes it impossible for us to succeed."

Perplexed, Oscar bit into his croissant and took another sip of coffee before responding. "Any idea why Darren wouldn't want Project One to be successful?"

"No clue," Diana answered.

"Okay. I'll do some digging. I appreciate your transparency. You mentioned challenges with the project team. Tell me about that," Oscar said.

"In general, it feels like the team is going through the motions rather than being truly committed and engaged," Diana began. "I thought the new plan would create the same excitement with them that you and I have, but it hasn't. I just feel like I'm missing something."

"I see. Well, keep in mind that the plan is just a plan," Oscar explained. "And because you co-created it, you have a vested interest in its success. It's a part of you. That's not true for project team members and other stakeholders. They all have their own history with Project One, some of which might not be pleasant. Understanding their different perspectives might be helpful. Remember when we talked about individual authenticity during our first meeting?"

Diana nodded, adding, "Oh my gosh, this financier is amazing!"

Smiling, Oscar continued. "Well, each team member's individual authenticity is on display, and it's influenced by their personal history and experience. Your job, as best you can, is to guide the team towards a shared connection that reflects the group. That would be the collective authenticity we discussed. It's the shared values and beliefs, and the expected actions and behaviors. In essence, it's the team's culture.

"That must shift if you want a different set of outcomes. Rather than simply facilitating the change phases, you must appeal to a deeper part of them. This is where your leadership shines. And I guarantee that the more authentic you are, the more success you'll have. To be clear, not everyone will change. But I believe more will change than you think. Have you had one-on-one time with any key players?"

"Honestly, I haven't, but you're making me think I probably should have," Diana replied. "We just sort of jumped back into the project. I haven't thought much about the project team changing. So, if I understand you correctly, the team members must first change their perspectives. Then we will be able to create different outcomes. And if I show up differently, I can influence the changes that take place within the team."

"Yep, that's it," Oscar affirmed. "Think about when you and I first met in my office to discuss Project One. You had no idea what to expect. I could sense your anxiety. And I attempted to reassure you by being transparent and vulnerable. I was clear about my thoughts and the role I saw us playing as we worked together.

"You might not have been aware of it, but you responded to that. You began to engage differently. Your energy and excitement around Project One completely shifted. You started thinking about how we could relaunch the project. That experience changed what you believed to be possible. That's the type of change you want to create with the project team. And honestly, I have to do the same with the steering committee and executive team."

"Ahhh ... that all makes sense," Diana mused. "But how, exactly, do I begin doing that?"

"You'll have to spend time with team members and dig a little deeper to understand their fears and concerns, and even what excites them. The more you can understand their view of the world, the more easily you can help them reshape it with regard to Project One and what's possible. I have a few tools that might be helpful," Oscar explained.

He brushed crumbs off the table into his empty mug as he said, "Question for you. When we planned our relaunch, did we ever talk about resistance and resonance?"

"You mentioned it briefly during our first meeting, but we never discussed it in detail," Diana replied.

Oscar grabbed a napkin and pulled a pen out of his inside jacket pocket, "Let me show you something. A few years ago, I read a research study about organizational transformations. It focused on how employees felt about the organization's current and future states. The study concluded that when evaluating the current state, employees fell into one of three groups: resonant, resistant, or dormant. Similarly, when evaluating the future state, employees fell into one of those same three groups. However, during change periods, employees might switch groups."

"That's intriguing," Diana said.

Oscar drew what appeared to be a partial grid and parabola on the napkin.

FIGURE 6. RESISTANCE AND RESONANCE SPECTRUM

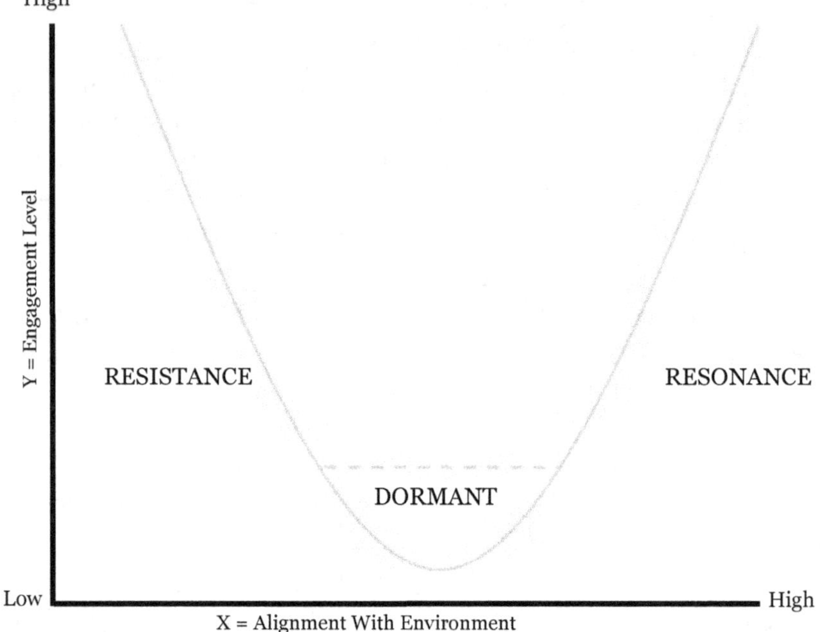

"Think about this," Oscar continued. "You have some employees who like the way things are. They feel good about the environment — the type of work they do, their manager, company culture, and so on. And these employees are engaged because they feel so aligned. These individuals are resonant," he said, pointing to the parabola's right side.

"This is because both their individual authenticity and collective authenticity are closely aligned. At the same time, in the same environment, you have some employees who'd like things to be different. Lisa comes to mind, right? These people are also engaged, but they feel like their individual authenticity and collective authenticity don't match. These employees are 'resistant.'

"Lastly, you have employees who are somewhat indifferent. They are less engaged and don't have a strong opinion about their relationship to the environment. We refer to them as 'dormant,'" Oscar said, looking up to make sure Diana was tracking. She nodded, so he continued.

"The study showed that these three dynamics coexist when it comes to the organization's current state. As change happens and the environment shifts, employees may find themselves staying in the same group — one of those three. Or, they might shift their perspective. Suddenly, someone like Lisa, who doesn't like the current state, is very excited about the future possibilities and how that will impact them. Maybe they report to a new manager, gain new responsibilities, or execute a new process.

"Regardless of the type of change, the key conclusion from the research was that for the change to happen, you must create enough momentum towards resonance. If too many employees, critical leaders, or influencers remain resistant, that energy will derail the change efforts," Oscar concluded.

"Wow! I've never had anyone explain change management that way," Diana said. "It intuitively makes a lot of sense. As I think back on my career, when projects failed, we tended to focus on root causes like poor execution. And there certainly might've been aspects of that. But we also always identified a level of active or passive resistance."

"I'm not surprised by that at all," Oscar said. "That's why understanding project team and key stakeholder perspectives is so important."

"But how do I do that? This is all new to me," Diana said.

"Developing that skill comes with time and experience," Oscar began, "but here is a little tool I developed that might help."

Oscar unlocked his phone, tapped the Photos app, and scrolled momentarily before enlarging a two-column table image.

"For the past five or six years, I've been tracking what I call leadership personas. They aren't based on any personality profiles or assessments. They're simply labels for some of the dominant leader behaviors I've seen over the years. I've found that understanding these core behavior patterns allows me to better understand a leader's perspective. More importantly, it allows me to understand how to relate to them when things are changing. It's not perfect, but it's been effective for me. Do you want to test it out?"

"Oh, of course!" Diana said with a sly smile.

"Okay! Take a minute to read through each persona and the bulleted descriptions," Oscar instructed.

Oscar gave her his phone. She handed it back a few moments later.

FIGURE 7. LEADERSHIP PERSONAS

Persona	Description
Truthteller	• People confide in this person, which allows them to gather information • Willing to speak the truth even when it's uncomfortable or unpopular
Fearful Leader	• Leads through fear because they are fearful
Untrusted Leader	• Lacks integrity, capacity, capability and/or reliability
Yes Person	• Always says "yes" to accomplishing tasks regardless of reasonableness or consequences
Catalyst	• Champion of change and highly open to a new set of possibilities
People's Champion	• Considers the impact to people first • Leads the organization's talent consciousness
Pessimist	• Identifies barriers for creating the future • Sees the downside in situations first
Egocentric	• Puts their own interests first • Doesn't see the impact on broader stakeholders
False Visionary	• Sees possibilities for the future that are unrealistic
Collaborator	• Master of stakeholder management who embraces multiple perspectives
Coach	• Leans into getting the best out of the team • Provides enterprise view that balances internal and external perspectives

Persona	Description
Executor	• Highly focused on getting things done with limited ability to think strategically
One-Trick Pony	• Master of single capability • Is challenged to stretch beyond their technical domain
Highly Authentic	• Leads with authenticity • Highly vulnerable and transparent • Considers the greatest good for all in decision making

"Do any of the personas jump out at you? Do you recognize any of them?" Oscar asked.

"Yes. Egocentric pops out first. I hate to say it, but that reminds me a little of Darren. Lisa is definitely a collaborator. Our partners in finance strike me as your one-trick ponies because they only care about the bottom line," Diana laughed.

Oscar chuckled.

"Because you're matching leaders here to personas so quickly, it sounds like these descriptions might help you think through how you can work with and even influence Project One stakeholders. Keep in mind, though, that these personas aren't perfect or even tested — they're only based on my experience. Also, leaders can demonstrate multiple personas. And lastly, they aren't about being good or bad," Oscar warned.

"You mentioned Darren representing the egocentric persona," he continued. "There may be times when that persona serves both Darren and the organization, so it's a plus. Also, you're only viewing Darren through a particular lens. When it comes to his team, who seem to genuinely like him, he could also be a people's champion. Just keep all that in mind."

"I will, Oscar. None of us is that simple. We're multidimensional, for sure," Diana observed.

"We're about out of time. How are you feeling?" Oscar asked, a note of concern in his voice.

"I feel much better now that we've talked. This was very helpful," Diana replied. "I'm still concerned about losing Lisa, but feel like I am better equipped to work with the project team in a way that will hopefully create positive momentum. It's about getting them to what you refer to as resonance."

"I'm glad to hear it, Diana," Oscar said. "I'm going to schedule time to meet with both Darren and Lisa separately. I need to get to the bottom of that dynamic. I also want to explore if there's anything we can do to keep Lisa at ABC. But let me text you the leadership personas image right now. We can circle back a week from today to do a quick check-in on how things are going."

He paused to send the image.

"That sounds great, Oscar," Diana replied. "I really appreciate your support."

"It's my pleasure. Now let's get an early start on the weekend," Oscar said.

"Chef and team, it's always a pleasure to be with you. I'll see you next week!" he said, waving with his free hand as he reached for the doorknob.

Back at the office, Diana began scheduling time to meet with key project team members the following week. She felt both excited and anxious about connecting with them in a different way.

Despite those mixed emotions, Diana fully trusted Oscar. She had never worked with an executive who invested so much time to help her become a better leader. She knew it would help change her and how she worked with others for the better.

5
Discovering Truth

OVER THE WEEKEND, Oscar contemplated how he might learn how his top leaders *truly* viewed Project One. Though he got an earful from Diana that Friday, he knew he needed to talk directly with Lisa and Darren. He texted both late Saturday afternoon to schedule conversations on Monday, starting with Lisa.

When she arrived at his office promptly at 9 a.m., Oscar was already sitting comfortably on the love seat in the middle of the office.

"Good morning, Lisa. Come on in. Can I get you anything? Coffee? Water?" Oscar asked.

"Happy Monday, Oscar! I'm all set, thank you," Lisa said, taking a seat across from him.

"So, I heard you're planning to leave ABC," Oscar began. "Diana mentioned it to me on Friday. I know you're a critical senior leader in our organization and on Project One specifically, so I hope you'll be willing to share what led to this decision and if there is anything we can do to change your mind."

"Yeah, Diana gave me a heads-up, so I wasn't surprised by your meeting invite," Lisa said. "I think it's just time for me to move on and try something different."

"Is that how you really feel? If I'm being honest, that sounds like a politically correct answer," Oscar said gently. "I guess I should expect that since we haven't spent much time together, and you don't know me that well. And if that's truly your final answer, so be it. But I want you to know that I understand there are underlying issues in the organization. There are behaviors that need to change if we want to be in business for another 75 years. My commitment to the board, our employees, and to you is to get to the bottom of our challenges so that we can build a better organization. However, if I don't know the issues, I can't address them."

Lisa sighed, but didn't respond.

Oscar broke the silence. "This is a safe space, Lisa. It's literally just you and me here. I promise that nothing you share will put you in a compromised position."

Taking a deep breath, Lisa began. "If I'm being totally honest, I don't think we have the right formula for a successful transformation."

"Tell me more," Oscar encouraged.

Lisa continued. "I've been at ABC for more than 20 years. Over the years, I've seen a consistent and discouraging behavior pattern. A new technology or capability hits the market, and someone in leadership suggests we pursue it. We end up trying to transform the organization with it, but never fully deliver the change and its benefits."

"This has happened every three to five years since I've been here," Lisa continued. "We've created a lot of complexity with these half-completed implementations and integrations. Just look at what is happening in fintech. We've consistently tried to develop cutting-edge technologies based on what fintechs are rolling out in the industry. Take the capabilities we attempted to roll out three years ago. We still haven't effectively capitalized on that investment. I'm hearing we are dumping the capability and might write it off completely as a loss."

"So why do you think ABC misses on these transformation efforts?" Oscar inquired.

"Well, I believe there are a few things," Lisa said thoughtfully as she stared down at her hands in her lap. "As an organization, we aren't as open to change as we might think. Our leadership team talks about change because it's in vogue. We want the outcomes it promises, but leaders don't seem to realize the change in mindset and behavior required for success. It feels like our antiquated culture and operating approach hold us back.

"Some of my friends at our competitors seem to have a very different experience when it comes to executing big and small changes. Here, on the other hand, we seem to be all over the place. It feels like we lack clarity. And I don't think we do a great job of holding leaders accountable. Take that fintech capability example. The leader who spearheaded that and was ultimately responsible for its performance has taken on a larger role in the organization despite completely missing the mark with it," Lisa said.

She paused, raising her eyes to Oscar's to see how he was reacting. He nodded. "Please continue. This truly is a safe space."

"This is common knowledge here," Lisa began again. "It's also common knowledge that said individual is very close with Robert, our CFO. We all know Robert and Michael are joined at the hip. So, no one wants to rock the boat."

"No accountability within the executive team?" Oscar clarified.

"Absolutely none!" Lisa exclaimed. "Look at how long the executive team has been in place. They all have at least 20 years of tenure, except for Phillip, our growth officer; Farouk, head of HR; and CTO Lora. All three have tried unsuccessfully to help move us towards a new type of organization. If you weren't aware, each of their predecessors retired on their own despite ABC's decade-long struggles. Some of us joke about becoming an executive so we can get a golden parachute, because no one ever leaves those jobs against their will. With strict enforcement of our mandatory retirement age of 65, most execs have simply aged out," she confided.

"This is very helpful context, Lisa. Thank you. Now, let's zero in on Project One and how that seems to be the tipping point for you. What are you seeing there?" Oscar asked.

"First, I think Project One is the right solution for ABC," Lisa continued. "Lora's technology team has built something special, and it could be revolutionary. Because of the complexity of our operations, moving to a single platform reduces costs, simplifies our infrastructure, and produces a best-in-class customer experience. However, I think the inherent resistance to change here, along with the lack of high-level accountability, will lead to us stumbling along for another two years without much to show for it."

"I know you have a vested interest in Project One's success, and your enthusiasm for it really is a breath of fresh air. But, as you know, I report to Darren, and he isn't exactly all in on this. Outwardly, he says the right things to show he supports it, but privately, he has been pretty clear with me and with some of my peers that he isn't jumping on board this particular transformation train."

Perplexed, Oscar asked, "I thought all our leaders understood the tough place we're in as a business. We must reduce costs and find ways to become more competitive. Any idea why Darren wouldn't support Project One?"

"To be honest with you, I'm not sure," Lisa began. "What I do know is that Darren is an ABC lifer. He has spent time in all the operations at the company. No one knows ABC operations like he does. His institutional knowledge is unmatched, and Michael and the rest of the executive team rely heavily on it. If we have operational issues that reach the CEO's desk, whether they're regulatory matters or customer complaints, Michael contacts Darren directly for explanations and resolutions — and for good reason, right? Darren has become an important figure when it comes to keeping the organization out of trouble."

Oscar replied, "I see. And what about you? Clearly, you have a deep understanding of and a strong view about what's happening. I think you could play an important role in helping us break this cycle. What would it take to get you to stay, Lisa?"

Caught off guard, Lisa answered, "I don't know, Oscar. I appreciate your interest in my perspective. Just being heard feels good, if I'm honest. I'm satisfied with my compensation for my role, but I could see myself doing more in the future. In my heart, I just want to see real change. We all do. Well, many of us do, anyway."

"I understand," Oscar responded. "How much time do I have to convince you to stay?"

Lisa thought for a moment. "I don't have to start the new job for two months, and I promised Darren I'd stick around here for the first half of that so we could manage a smooth transition. I planned on using the second 30 days for some much-needed R and R," Lisa said.

"Are you open to finding a way to stay here, if we have a solid plan for turning some of this around?" he asked.

Lisa hesitated, then said, "Sure. The only reason I'm leaving is because I'm tired of how we get mired in the status quo to the point where I feel I can't make a difference. If you can show me how we might turn this around, I'll consider it fairly. I'm always ready for the right challenge," she smiled.

"Great! Can you give me a week to make some progress, then we'll circle back? And maybe keep this just between us and, if you'd like, Diana?" Oscar asked.

Lisa nodded as she replied, "Sure. I'm happy to meet with you for an update then."

"Great! I'll ask Shannon to schedule a meeting. And thank you for being so transparent with me, Lisa. I know that takes courage. I'm hopeful we will get to a different place," Oscar said, standing up.

After seeing Lisa out, Oscar returned to his desk to think about what he had just learned and how it might influence his meeting with Darren later that day. After a few moments, he pulled a notebook from a desk drawer and began capturing his thoughts. He wanted to be careful to maintain Lisa's confidence while addressing the potential disconnect with Darren.

Later that day, Darren joined Oscar in his office. Oscar showed him to the center seating area, then sat in his favorite spot on the loveseat. Darren sat across from him in the same chair Lisa had chosen earlier that day.

"Darren, I appreciate you taking the time to meet on short notice," Oscar began. "I wanted to connect with you about Project One and get your thoughts on how things are going, especially since you benefit the most from the initiative."

"No problem at all, Oscar," Darren replied. "Overall, I think Project One is going just fine. Diana has done a great job of pulling the team together for it. Lisa from my team has been running point because she runs credit card customer service operations, and they are going live first. I have full trust in her leadership."

Oscar got to the point of the meeting quickly. "I'm glad to hear that. Diana expressed some concerns about the project team getting on board and mentioned Lisa has resigned and will be leaving in about 30 days. She would be a big loss for ABC and Project One, yeah?"

"Yes, Lisa talked to me about that late last week. I haven't shared the news with anyone yet because I'm thinking about the best strategy for replacing her," Darren answered defensively.

"She appears to be a top performer and has been here a long time. Why is she leaving?" Oscar asked.

Darren, who knew the CEO trusted him, began feeling uncomfortable. It had been a long time since he'd felt even remotely challenged or pushed by anyone, he thought, and while Oscar seemed relaxed and nonconfrontational, Darren felt threatened. He paused momentarily before responding. "She is looking for a new growth opportunity and more money. She's never worked anywhere else, and you know how it is. It's tough to be compensated at the market rate if you've worked at the same place your entire career. We'll be fine, especially since this gives me an opportunity to elevate someone on Lisa's team. I have someone in mind already."

Rather than accepting that at face value, Oscar probed. "It seems like this would be a difficult time to lose a leader we consider top talent. Do you think she is worth retaining?"

Darren paused, wondering if Oscar knew more than he was letting on. But before he could respond, Oscar continued.

"I want to be completely transparent with you, Darren. Diana raised a concern about Lisa's departure and how it puts Project One at risk. I tend to agree with her, especially since the credit card customer service operations will be first to transition to the new technology. In addition, Lisa appears to be something of an operations rockstar. From what I've seen already, she has developed a high-performing team and demonstrated truly strategic thinking.

"All that shows up in her HR performance scorecard as well as in my interactions with her," Oscar continued. "Management seems to think highly of her, and she clearly understands what ABC needs to do to be successful in the future. My gut tells me we should carefully consider what losing a leader of Lisa's caliber would mean during a time when the organization is struggling to survive. My concern is if top talent leaves, and we don't have a retention strategy for the folks whose values and capabilities align with where we want to be, we will end up with a domino effect, not to mention the more immediate impact on her team's morale. It also clearly puts Project One at risk," he said.

Darren leaned away from Oscar, clearly put off by what he saw as a challenge to his leadership and authority.

"I'll take that under advisement, Oscar," Darren said, starting to rise.

"As it relates to Project One," Oscar continued, leaving Darren no choice but to sit back down, "I've started to dig a little deeper. I'm concerned there are still disconnects across the organization in terms of support. I am working with the executive team to get us on the same page, but I've picked up that you might not be a fan of what we're trying to accomplish here. Is that true? You're a critical stakeholder, so it's important we are in sync."

"I'm going to be honest with you, Oscar," a clearly agitated Darren began. "I think Project One is a good thing. It's a cool artificial intelligence technology, but it's not necessary. ABC has survived for more than 75 years without it. We have leaders, like me, who know a lot about our industry and understand how our business works. I'm confident we will rebound from the challenges we're up against. This is what we do. We dig in when times are hard, and we always emerge on the other side."

Oscar calmly responded, "I understand where you're coming from, Darren. I do. But we are in different times. Financial services technology is rapidly evolving, which leaves some of our businesses in the operational Stone Age. We must build the future now by modernizing. During site visits, I've seen thousands of manual processes in customer service and the back office that rely on a single subject matter expert to execute. This is frightening. We've relied on people who grew up here to keep us afloat when we should be either sharing that expertise more broadly or taking advantage of technology that can automate those processes and free that talent up to perform higher-value work.

"Unfortunately, that means we haven't scaled operations and can't consistently deliver on our brand promise to customers. And from my experience, I'm sure it makes it very difficult for new employees to come in and learn their jobs," he said.

Oscar moved to his desk and grabbed a sheet of paper with last month's HR retention report metrics. He handed it to Darren, who saw that Oscar had highlighted the section showing that more than 90% of the company's attrition came from employees with less than two years at the firm.

"I think you raise some good points," Darren said, looking up from the report. "But it doesn't change my belief about our future. Besides, if we implement this new technology, what does that mean to the leaders and employees who know the business so well? It sounds like they risk becoming obsolete."

"We are a large organization and will still need a large workforce to serve our customers," Oscar reassured. "Yes, some jobs will go away, and new jobs with different skill sets will emerge. But the more we distribute knowledge, the more effective we will be at serving customers. The new technology allows for that. In an organization our size, relying on one or two individuals' expertise to execute processes isn't a sustainable solution. It's expensive, inefficient, and impossible to scale. We must change if we want to survive into the future.

"ABC is at a tipping point. I'd even argue the tipping point was several years ago when Project One was first initiated. Unfortunately, we are behind, and time is of the essence," he said, leaning forward with intensity.

"Oscar, with all due respect, you're still learning our business. You don't know how everything works. We go through these periods occasionally. My leaders and I know what's best because we've done this many, many times before. And I think Michael would also agree with my assessment," Darren added, playing what he thought was a trump card.

Oscar was momentarily taken aback by Darren's lack of perspective and inability to grasp how changes outside the company have an impact inside it. Having worked in several organizations and industries where middle and senior leaders incorporated external factors into strategic planning, Oscar knew how important this larger world view was to success in a rapidly evolving marketplace. Was this Darren's biggest blind spot?

Still, he didn't hold this against Darren, who was a product of his environment. It reflected how Darren learned to lead there, and it had worked for him — until now. Darren was simply continuing to embrace behaviors he had always been rewarded for. And Oscar appreciated how his new, different view would feel threatening to his colleague.

The two leaders went back and forth for the next several minutes discussing Lisa's impending departure, the pros and cons of Project One, and ABC's overall health. Once both realized they were at an impasse, they agreed to stop and reconvene in a few days.

Knowing that Darren's resistance meant he might not fit with the company's new direction, Oscar felt a surge of compassion for his colleague as he sat behind his desk. Throughout the conversation, Darren's emotions were overriding the balanced, rational approach he had become known for. It was a classic example of reaction versus response.

It was critical that Darren supported Project One if it was going to succeed, so Oscar knew he had to be thoughtful about his next move. As a highly authentic leader, he was well-versed in how difficult decisions could be unpopular, even when the outcomes help promise a healthy future for the company and its employees.

Thinking ahead to Thursday's meeting with Michael and Farouk to discuss the corporation's talent strategy, he added a last-minute agenda topic for the three executives: discussing his conversations with Lisa and Darren.

6
Locks and Keys

ARMED WITH OSCAR's leadership personas, Diana spent the first half of the week meeting with all the Project One key stakeholders. She needed to understand whether each leader felt they had the right resources, along with enough support from her. Most importantly, Diana wanted to know each leader's perspective, especially around ABC's current state and the future Project One would create for the company.

By mid-afternoon Wednesday, confident she had the full picture, Diana treated herself to a reward for managing the oftentimes frank, sometimes surprising conversations with neutrality: one of Chef Andre's deliciously decadent pastries before her end-of-the-day meeting with Oscar.

As she walked through the patisserie's bright yellow entrance, Diana was startled by the staff's personal greeting. "Diiaannaa!!!!" called Andre and one of his servers. She laughed in surprise.

"It's so good to see you again, Diana," Andre said. "How are you? And what can we get for you this time?"

Diana felt almost giddy as she scanned the pastries in the glass case.

"The almond croissants just came out of the oven and are as fresh as can be," Andre said coaxingly.

"That sounds lovely, Chef," Diana replied. "I'll take one of them along with a decaf coffee for here."

"Perfect!" Andre exclaimed. "Would you like to take Monsieur Oscar's seat by the window? I'll bring your order to you."

Diana nodded and walked to the window table she and Oscar had shared the previous Friday. A few minutes later, Andre placed her order alongside her laptop, glancing at her computer screen as he did so.

"Ahhh, leadership personas?" he asked.

Surprised, Diana replied, "Yes. Yes, it is! How do you know about these?"

"Oscar shared them with me, hmmm, probably three or four years ago," Andre said. "He is teaching you about authenticity, no?"

"I'm so sorry," Diana replied. "I am so confused right now. Did you and Oscar work together? How do you know about this?"

"No, we never worked together per se," Andre replied, taking the chair opposite his new friend. "Oscar was more of an advisor. I met him several years ago when I was executive chef at the French bistro Le Salon on the other side of town."

"Wow!" Diana gasped. "I heard that place is amazing! I remember when it won a Michelin Star. My friends and I have tried to get a reservation, but it's at least a six-month wait. I can't believe you were the executive chef there. But wait … why would you leave a restaurant like that?"

Before answering, Andre took off his chef's hat and placed it on the empty chair next to him. "Well, if I'm being totally honest with you, I felt like I couldn't be myself there. As a kid growing up outside of Paris, I learned to cook in my grand-mère's kitchen. She taught me so much. She's why I chose culinary school. I dreamed of being an executive chef at an exceptional restaurant that served food people would travel to experience.

"And that happened when I joined Le Salon," he

continued. "The restaurant was extremely successful — more than I ever imagined I'd have the right to experience. But with that success came a new set of expectations.

"A large restaurant group acquired Le Salon. The new owners brought a different vision, one that pushed for a higher volume of the status quo rather than continuing our tradition of creatively experimenting in ways that could produce an even better, more exciting menu for diners.

"Under the new management, my culinary creativity and emotional connection to the food began to dim. My day-to-day became a rinse-and-repeat routine that produced a higher volume of top-quality food and service but lacked creativity. The goal was no longer to wow our patrons with meals they had never experienced before — especially so close to home — but to continually find ways to maintain quality while serving more people. I felt like I was no longer evolving as a chef, and all of it left me exhausted.

"I met Oscar at my lowest point when he was a consultant. He overheard my conversation with the restaurant group owner in a coffee shop. My frustration was obvious, so after the owner left, Oscar literally sat down next to me and asked if there was anything he could do to help. That day changed my life," Andre said.

Clearly intrigued, Diana asked, "So, what happened? How do you know about the personas?"

"I told Oscar about the situation, which included that I really wanted to cook in a way that felt authentic to who I was," Andre said. "Oscar helped me see that I wasn't aligned with the restaurant group and where it was taking Le Salon. Basically, my individual authenticity didn't match their collective authenticity. When he explained it to me, it made perfect sense. And he pointed out two clear options: I could attempt to influence the environment so it matches who I am, or I could leave. In the first scenario, I'd have to talk with the restaurant group owner and explain what I needed to feel like myself and to continue to be inspired.

"Oscar and I exchanged phone numbers, and I thought about our initial conversation for a week before reaching out to him to discuss it a bit more. He was happy to help! During our first meeting, I explained what I thought I wanted as an outcome, and Oscar pushed me to get more specific about what being fully resonant at work could look like.

"I struggled with that for a few more weeks because I only had one frame of reference — my Le Salon experience — and my beliefs about my new reality. It took three additional sessions to just get clear about what I truly wanted. That was a powerful exercise that helped me see how my limiting beliefs kept me from envisioning what was possible.

"Oscar eventually explained the leadership personas and how I could use them to understand who did and didn't support the new direction we were going," Andre said. He went on to tell Diana the key players were the restaurant group owner, Le Salon's owner, who, as part of the deal, became a key leader in the restaurant group, and several other group executives.

"Using Oscar's model, I met with each to understand their perspectives and determine how I wanted to proceed. The sessions with Oscar allowed me to approach each leader with so much clarity. During the leadership meetings, I learned that nearly all the leaders were on board with a new vision for the restaurant. At the same time, some of the executives saw value in my vision for the restaurant, and their perspectives shifted a bit.

"That was my first experience with Oscar's 'locks and keys' concept. Both owners were 'locked' on the future they envisioned, and my efforts to shift their perspectives were unsuccessful. Ultimately, I decided it was best for me to leave. Oscar helped me through that entire evaluation process and my transition."

"Wait!" Diana exclaimed. "What's the 'locks and keys' concept? You kind of lost me there," Diana said.

"Oh, Oscar hasn't explained that to you yet?" Andre asked. "Well, every person has a perspective, right? That perspective is grounded in their beliefs. When someone has a strong belief about something, that individual is a 'lock.' A 'key' is a person or experience that has the potential to unlock that strong perspective and change it."

Andre pointed at Diana's laptop screen. "Think about your leadership personas and the names you wrote next to each. Oscar would probably tell you that the next step is thinking about which person on that list is a lock and which is a potential key, because with big changes, you'll need more than one key to unlock perspectives. Sometimes, your job is to influence others in ways that turn them into keys that unlock others.

"You've been at ABC for a while, right? You know that some of these leaders have worked together a long time and developed strong bonds. For those who are locked, hearing your message from another voice they trust can sometimes create the spark needed to shift their perspective. In essence, understanding the network and who else can be keys to others' locks can be powerful. As those locks open, you build momentum towards your goal, which is resonance with the change you want."

"My mind is completely blown!" Diana exclaimed. "This is so fascinating! You used this approach in the hospitality industry?"

"Yes, and it worked quite well," Andre explained. "It saved me so much time and energy because I wasn't pushing a boulder uphill, as you say here. Most of the restaurant group leaders were not interested in altering the plan in a way that preserved the restaurant's unique personality.

And the top leaders certainly weren't open to it, even if it meant losing me, their top chef. And that's okay. I don't judge them for that. It just meant I wasn't aligned with them, and if I wanted to be fulfilled and a more authentic version of myself, I needed to leave."

"Is that when you decided to open this place?" Diana wondered.

"Actually, no. I liked the consistency, comfort, and security that come with working for someone else. I became another restaurant's executive chef. I understood very quickly, though, that I still didn't have the creative freedom I wanted. During one of our coffee sessions, Oscar encouraged me to think about why cooking for others was so meaningful to me, and how I could experience that every day when I'm working."

Curious, Diana asked, "What did you come up with?"

"Well, growing up in France, my family was poor," Andre began. "So, as I helped my grand-mère cook, she often improvised based on the ingredients we could afford that day. It was magical to see her turn nothing into something that tasted so good. She told me once, too, that cooking was her way of expressing love to our family. Here, I think you say, 'Food is my love language.' My grand-mère put her heart and soul into everything she prepared for us," he said, getting up to pour Diana another cup of decaf.

"That dedication. That resilience. That love. All of it led me to become a chef. And Grand-mère's affinity for sweets is what inspired me to eventually open this place. It's a space where I can be the most authentic version of myself. Everyone here wants to prepare top-quality pastries and serve customers with love and positivity. I embrace their creative energy by encouraging them to try different things, whether it's what they bake or how they present it."

Andre pointed across the room. "Gabrielle, right over there, is the one who suggested getting to know our customers so we could greet them by name. So … it might not surprise you to learn that she's studying marketing at City University! Watching our returning customers' faces when we call their name brings her so much joy! And each of those interactions is a reminder of who Gabrielle is and her contributions to this place.

"George, who is taking that customer's order, is a finance major. He has helped us turn a profit more quickly by implementing new financial systems and controls. He's shown me how to manage our inventory with precision so there's little waste.

"All of us are contributing in different ways towards the same goal. Their individual authenticity matches the collective authenticity of Patisserie et Mes Amies. And we share in the collective success," he explained.

"In truth, not every employee has felt that connection," Andre continued. "Like any business, we have turnover. Departures are never acrimonious, though, because I want them to find a position that feels authentic to them. Oscar gets some credit for that — he had a way of getting me to lead with both my heart and my head, not one or the other. And the good news is that some former employees who have stopped by for pastries have confirmed that they're thriving in a different environment, too, which feels validating for all of us. Like me, they've found that working for an organization that they feel aligned with is a very different experience from just 'working.'"

"And you learned all this from Oscar?" Diana asked.

Andre grinned. "Well, I learned it from myself. Oscar was the catalyst. He was the key to my lock, shining the light so that I could see things a little differently."

"Well, this coffee break was much more than I anticipated," Diana laughed. "Thank you for sharing your fascinating story with me, Andre. And by the way, I love what you're doing here."

Andre smiled as he stood up. "It's my pleasure, Diana. I assume Oscar has also talked about manifested authenticity, no? Our pastries, coffees, and the entire experience here reflect the collective Patisserie et Mes Amies team. If you like it, it's because something about it aligns with who you are. Now, enjoy the rest of your day, and good luck with your leadership personas! If I can help at all, let me know. And your next coffee is on the house for listening to my story," he winked.

He disappeared back into the kitchen. Rather than return to the office, Diana continued working at the sweet-smelling shop for the next hour before walking back to ABC headquarters for her meeting with Oscar.

When Diana arrived at his office, Oscar was staring at the city skyline outside his window, his mind seemingly elsewhere. This wasn't unusual for him lately. When he wasn't in meetings, Oscar constantly considered the necessary balance between accepted, day-to-day operations and the need for ABC to change. The two very different perspectives always seemed to be in tension with one another. He could see it within his direct reports and across the executive team as leaders struggled to determine whether their priority was maintaining the known — and therefore safe status quo — or delivering transformational change.

Oscar turned from the window when he heard Diana enter. "Come, sit down, Diana," he smiled.

Sensing his preoccupation, Diana asked, "Is this still a good time? You seemed deep in thought."

"Oh, yes, now is perfect," Oscar reassured her as he sat on the love seat. "Let's talk about the leadership personas and how your meetings with stakeholders are going."

Diana turned her laptop towards Oscar as she said, "I've met with everyone and added a few columns and notes to the table I created."

Oscar reviewed the file for a minute before saying, "This looks pretty good. Your notes are thorough. And you've met with everyone already?"

Clearly proud, Diana said, "Yes, and I have a strong sense of who might be a lock and who might be a key."

At first surprised by Diana's response, Oscar then grinned. "I saw you walking back to the building from the direction of Patisserie et Mes Amies just now. You spoke with Chef Andre, didn't you?"

Diana laughed. "He noticed the leadership personas on my laptop when he brought my order — and holy cow, have you tried his almond croissant? He told me how you helped him choose between staying at the restaurant after it was acquired and pursuing a path where he could feel more authentic. It was a powerful story. And it's amazing to see him thriving now."

"And I'll bet you thought you'd be there just long enough for a coffee break!" Oscar laughed. "Andre is a great example of how to understand and figure out locks and keys. And, at the end of the day, you won't be able to open every lock. We need to appreciate and accept that part of the change process. Acceptance is not about getting everyone on board. It's about agreeing to move forward, fully aware of where we are aligned and where we aren't.

"So, we continue to support the work even if at times we feel like we aren't getting exactly what we want. But we agree that the greater good we are trying to achieve supersedes our own individual needs. That's why understanding different perspectives is so critical. As leaders, one of our most difficult tasks is determining whether someone who is resisting and seemingly unwilling to change has the potential to become disruptive enough to put the entire initiative at risk. That's part of what you and I will have to assess."

"Ahhh, someone like Darren," Diana said quietly,

almost under her breath.

Oscar perked up. "What do you mean?"

Diana was reluctant to be completely honest with Oscar. Still, he had earned a fair amount of trust, and she wanted him to fully understand what he was up against. Her success depended on it, too, after all.

"There has been some scuttlebutt about Darren telling a few people that he wasn't happy with a conversation you two had about Project One," Diana began. "I got an earful directly from him, too, because he knows I have concerns about the initiative. You and I have talked about them, and we'll figure it out. But Darren? It sounds like he isn't going down without a fight. And he believes Michael will back him if there is a need to choose between, um, him … or you. Is there anything I can do to ease the tension?"

Oscar responded quickly, "No, no. I understand Darren's frustration, and I'm sure we will find a resolution for that. There's not much you can do there, but you can help by continuing to observe. Watch behaviors as we go through this change. Note when people begin lashing out and getting others involved, because that helps us gauge the overall resistance level. When it happens, talk to them with compassion. They're struggling to find a perspective that feels better than where they are.

"It will help to think about Andre's story when this comes up, too. Though it may look a little different, he ultimately went from being resistant to resonant when he chose to leave Le Salon and do something else. Sometimes moving out of resistance requires us to leave the environment because we will never feel aligned. Sometimes we can get there on our own, and sometimes we can't," Oscar explained.

Moving to the small conference table on the other side of the office, he said, "Let's shift gears and talk through your leadership personas. Please put them up on the big screen."

Joining him at the table, Diana connected the HDMI cable to the laptop so her leadership personas table and leadership notes were on the large room screen by the table.

FIGURE 8. LEADERSHIP PERSONAS AND NOTES

Persona	Description	Leader
Truthteller	• People confide in this person, which allows them to gather information • Willing to speak the truth even when it's uncomfortable or unpopular	Erik
Fearful Leader	• Leads through fear because they are fearful	Bijal
Untrusted Leader	• Lacks integrity, capacity, capability and/or reliability	
Yes Person	• Always says "yes" to accomplishing tasks regardless of reasonableness or consequences	Lena, Brian
Catalyst	• Champion of change and highly open to a new set of possibilities	Oscar, Lora
People's Champion	• Considers the impact to people first • Leads the organization's talent consciousness	Farouk, Anastasia
Pessimist	• Identifies barriers for creating the future • Sees the downside in situations first	Bijal
Egocentric	• Puts their own interests first • Doesn't see the impact on broader stakeholders	Michael?, Robert?
False Visionary	• Sees possibilities for the future that are unrealistic	Michael?
Collaborator	• Master of stakeholder management who embraces multiple perspectives	Diana, Lisa
Coach	• Leans into getting the best out of the team • Provides enterprise view that balances internal and external perspectives	Oscar
Executor	• Highly focused on getting things done	Diana, Fernando
One-Trick Pony	• Master of single capability • Is challenged to stretch beyond their technical domain	Robert
Highly Authentic	• Leads with authenticity • Highly vulnerable and transparent • Considers the greatest good for all in decision making	Oscar

Note: Additional personas are "The Know It All," "Tethered to the Past," and "Bandwagon Jumper."

"It looks like you have a really good sense of where you think leaders are as it relates to Project One," Oscar began. "Let's test what Andre shared with you about locks and keys and how that may influence your approach going forward."

Wanting to impress her boss, Diana said quickly, "I think everyone I have marked as resistant is currently a lock."

"Makes sense," Oscar acknowledged.

She continued. "Not everyone who is in resonance is a key, but some will be. I know I'm probably not the key to every lock here either, so I plan to ask the resonant team members who are highly regarded, or who work closely with those who are resisting, to discuss Project One with them. If we understand the barriers creating resistance while continuing to raise awareness of the 'why' behind the project, we might be able to move some of them into resonance. Obviously, I will do my part to support the entire team."

Oscar applauded Diana's understanding. "That's very good, Diana. Let me ask you a question. When you see some of these leadership personas, like the fearful leader or the pessimist, what's your initial response to the label?"

Diana looked confused. "I'm not sure I understand your question."

"When you think about a pessimistic leader compared to a highly authentic leader, do you evaluate them differently?" he asked by way of explanation.

"Maybe?" Diana answered, beginning to work through her own confusion. "I probably would feel more aligned or connected to a highly authentic leader than I would a pessimist."

"Okay, that's getting closer to where I'm heading," Oscar encouraged. "So, how do you show up when you're interacting with someone you see as a pessimist?"

"Honestly, I probably avoid them because I'm not much of a pessimist," Diana laughed. "I mean, who wants to be around negativism all the time?"

Oscar sat silently for a moment.

Suddenly unsure of herself, Diana asked, "Was that a trick question? I feel like I just fell into a trap."

"No, no, it's not a trap. That's not my style," Oscar smiled. "But it is an important aspect that I want to highlight. When you review these leadership personas and relate them to the people you work with, it's important to avoid judging the outward behaviors as 'good' or 'bad.' Every perspective adds value because it contributes to the collective whole. And there's a reason leaders show up the way they do. Sometimes it has nothing to do with the job.

"I'll give you an example," Oscar continued. "A few minutes ago, you said Darren was resistant. What leadership persona do you have assigned to him?"

Diana turned toward the table on the screen. "Let's see ... I have him as egocentric, tethered to the past, and fearful," Diana said.

"Okay, and I don't disagree with your assessment," Oscar said. "Now, you have worked with Darren for the past several years. Think back to a time when you felt like you experienced the best version of him. Do you remember?"

Diana thought for a moment before saying she did.

"During that time — and only that time — which leadership personas would you have used to describe him?"

"Hmmm ... I see where you're going with this," a surprised Diana said. "He was probably a people's champion, coach, and maybe even a catalyst."

"And do you think Darren was in resonance or resistance

during that time?" Oscar prodded.

Diana paused for a moment as she thought. "He was probably resonant. In fact, I know he was. That was around the time he was being promoted. He was so excited."

"Perfect!" Oscar exclaimed. "My point is that we constantly reveal parts of ourselves, especially when things are changing, because that's when our status quo is disrupted. Our emotions are a response to that disruption. And it's important not to judge that. Trust me, this is not always easy. But the more objective you can be about the personas, accepting that leaders will feel real emotions that will manifest in different ways, the better able you will be to uncover and explore the underlying beliefs that are reflected in what you're seeing," Oscar said.

"Let me give you another example. The leader who is tethered to the past may not want to change because they helped build the current state, or it's linked in their mind to recognition from that period. Maybe they've tied their professional self-esteem to it. Or a bandwagon jumper may agree with the popular opinion because they don't want to be rejected or seen as an outlier. Bandwagon jumping is a protection mechanism.

"These aren't absolutes, but examples to get you thinking about why certain personas exist within the project team. Once you start peeling back the layers with each individual, you will be better equipped to understand potential beliefs that contribute to their resistance. That's the key to moving them into a situation where what you're doing actually resonates with them."

Diana replied, hesitantly, "I'm not sure I'm equipped to do that, Oscar. That sounds like something a psychologist or a coach would do. Isn't HR responsible for that type of work?"

"I understand what you're saying," Oscar replied. "You might feel a little intimidated by this, but I'm here to help.

How about this? What if I sit in on the first conversation you have with someone you think you might be able to unlock? Then we can debrief after, and I'll share my thoughts and observations with you. How does that sound?"

Still not convinced she could do this, Diana responded, "Yes, we could try that."

"My point is that in most cases, the thing people are concerned about is very rarely the true barrier that is creating resistance," Oscar said. "I'm confident you will develop a deeper understanding and appreciation for this soon, very soon.

"And really, Diana, you are doing a great job. I especially appreciate that you're open to this new way of leading change. I truly think this will have a bigger impact on you and the project team than you understand right now. You will be the key to many, many locks."

Oscar glanced at his watch. "It's getting late, so let's wrap up."

While Diana packed her laptop into her leather tote, Oscar moved to his desk and tucked a few items from his desk into a backpack before they walked to the elevator together.

Despite her anxiety, Diana remained excited about the new skills she was developing while working with Oscar. And Oscar continued to be pleased with his new colleague's openness and willingness to learn. Their conversation today reinforced his optimism about Project One, although he knew next week's meeting with CEO Michael and CHRO Farouk would play an important role in how he and Diana moved forward.

7
Tough Decisions

THE FOLLOWING MONDAY afternoon, Oscar and Farouk joined Michael in his office to discuss ABC's corporate talent strategy, starting with Oscar's late addition: a discussion about Lisa and Darren. Oscar knew from experience that pre-meetings before critical discussions often helped make important conversations more productive, so a few days earlier, he gave Farouk a heads-up on his conversations with Lisa and Darren. Oscar wasn't trying to create an alliance with the HR head that could oppose Michael or catch him off guard. Instead, and especially as a new executive in the organization, Oscar needed to understand the human resource implications of any potential key leadership changes. He looked to Farouk for objective guidance.

Farouk kicked off the meeting with Michael. "To best use our time this morning, I took the liberty of updating our agenda. We'll discuss Oscar's conversations with Lisa and Darren first. I think that is a priority. If we have time, we'll get to why we need to re-envision the ABC talent strategy."

Looking intrigued, Michael replied, "That sounds good. Who wants to start?"

Farouk looked at Oscar, who said, "You and Farouk are well aware of the work Diana and I are doing to drive the revised Project One plan. As expected, Diana has hit some early roadblocks when working to get some leaders on board. After her meetings with these key players, we worked on a plan that would improve their alignment with Project One and its goals. We are optimistic about it.

"However, my biggest concern is that Darren isn't on board with it. This is odd because he benefits the most from it. I've discovered that he has been undermining our work behind the scenes. This is a big problem for both the project team and me. Lisa has shared in confidence that while she and her team are on board with Project One, Darren's lack of support is making it difficult for them to implement it successfully. As a result, Lisa gave her 30-day notice last week and plans to join Old World Bank, which, as you know, is our biggest competitor. I believe the entire project is at risk if we lose Lisa, and Darren isn't open to changing how we do things."

Before Oscar could continue, Michael said, "I don't understand, Oscar. Why wouldn't Darren support the project?"

"Last week, Darren and I discussed both Lisa's pending departure and Project One at length," Oscar began. "He didn't say it exactly this way, but Darren fears he and others who built their careers at ABC will become less relevant as new technology taps into and shares the institutional knowledge they've acquired over the years.

"Believe me, I understand that concern. However, we will never scale if our senior people continue to lead in the same ways. Darren thinks ABC can ride out the financial challenges we face by doing things the way they've always been done. That seems to conflict with the urgency the executive team has been openly sharing about the state of the organization.

"Despite my best efforts to help Darren see the positive potential, we landed at an impasse. Lisa, on the other hand, sees the bigger picture and appears to role-model the leadership behaviors we want for the future. She has challenged Darren, so rather than try to keep her, he's planning to replace her by promoting someone on his team. My guess is Lisa's replacement will be someone more like-minded with Darren. In my opinion, that would be catastrophic for ABC. And I probably don't have to remind you that you brought me in as a change agent, starting with Project One."

Michael could see where this was heading. Crossing his arms as he leaned back in his chair, he asked, "So, what are you suggesting?"

"If we are going to successfully deliver Project One, our top leaders must be on board. I can't keep Darren as the head of operations if he isn't open to new ways of doing things. People who resist change create resistance for others, which is exactly what Lisa and her team have experienced. Removing Darren as operations head means his direct reports, who are already aligned with the plan, will be in a better position to execute it. My understanding is they all see the technology's promise, are excited about it, and want to implement it."

Turning to Farouk, Michael asked, "Have we ever fired any of our top leaders? I can't think of a time when we've done that. It seems so counter to our culture."

Farouk answered, "I've only been here seven years, but during that time, we haven't removed anyone on the executive team, or their direct reports, for that matter. Well, wait, maybe we *have* laid off a few higher-level folks when we've reorganized and had to reduce the workforce, but that's been rare."

Oscar jumped in. "Michael, I know this isn't easy for a company like ABC. That's why I don't make the recommendation lightly. I get it, believe me. But if we want to be more profitable, we must make different decisions and encourage different behaviors. Otherwise, we will get more of the same. I hate to make an example of any leader, but Darren departing ABC sends a signal.

"And the reality is that if the company is committed to becoming a new organization and Darren isn't aligned with that direction, he won't be happy here because he will resist the changed environment. And there's a negative ripple effect. Leaders under Darren will try to appease him while they're trying to support a new way of doing things. I've seen this story play out exactly this way plenty of times. People often sacrifice what they know is right to be aligned with their managers. That happens in part because of the incentive structures. We are compensated based on how we perform, and our direct managers have significant input on performance ratings, bonuses, and promotions."

Oscar continued, "To avoid creating a self-preservation-focused, fearful environment that will interfere with our work to deliver Project One, we must figure out who supports the new direction and who doesn't. Those who don't? We'll work with them to understand their perspectives and try to get them on board. They will still have the power to choose whether they are aligned with where we're going and how we'll get there, or with our old ways of working — we can't make that decision for them. But we can offer support and encouragement. Ultimately, we must be deliberate about who will lead us into a smarter and more profitable future.

"In the short term, I suggest offering Darren a generous severance package. We could even contract with him as a transition consultant for a while if he's open to that. Being able to tap into his institutional knowledge would be a definite plus. Regardless, the operational leaders who report to him can report to me for now. From a talent perspective, Lisa is highly regarded, and I'd like to try to keep her. Her credit card customer service operations division will be the first to transition to the new technology, and I think the process will take too long without her. I'd like to match the offer she received from Old World Bank.

"Lastly, if we can keep Lisa, as we complete Project One and I work more closely with her, I'll evaluate her for broader operations roles. I think she is talented enough to take on more responsibility," he concluded.

"Very good," Michael said. "I'll leave it to you both to work out the details of Darren's severance package and Lisa's retention offer. Working with Darren as a consultant is an excellent idea. Let me know if you need me to be involved in any way, especially if he's too angry to consider a consulting offer. Otherwise, I have confidence in both of you. And I'm here if there is any fallout."

Michael knew these were the right decisions for ABC. Oscar's explanation made him wonder why *he* hadn't thought about leadership this way since taking over as CEO. He was beginning to admire Oscar's clarity, decisiveness, and overall leadership. He grudgingly began to understand why board chair Erik had been so adamant about installing Oscar on the executive team.

After a brief discussion about talent strategy, Farouk began wrapping things up. "Okay, we have our next steps. Oscar, I'll schedule time for us to work through the details and communication plan. And the three of us can circle back as needed. Thank you both."

At the elevators, Farouk looked at Oscar and said quietly, "That went much better than I expected. And this is a big decision. Good for you."

"Thanks, Farouk," Oscar replied. "I think we all want what's best for the company. And sometimes our emotions stop us from making the decisions that will move us forward. I could almost see Michael mentally running through his history with Darren. At the same time, he knows this place won't be around if we don't make big changes. And it can be hard to make those decisions when there's a lot of history between people. What he did just now shows real leadership, don't you think?"

Oscar continued musing as they stepped into the empty elevator. "Hopefully, people will understand these decisions aren't judgments against anyone. I'll be clear about that when I speak with Darren. Ultimately, if he doesn't feel he can be aligned with our approach, he will be better off finding a new environment where he *does*. And we can help him discover that.

"Unfortunately, the people who got us here won't get us there if they don't want to change. That's the beauty of leading during change, though. We tap into experiences and perspectives for the sake of creating something new. To do that, our leaders must be open to that possibility."

"That's astute," Farouk smiled. "If I haven't mentioned it yet, I'm glad you're here to help us create a new future for the business."

"I appreciate that, Farouk. I'm glad we're working together, too," Oscar replied. "I've got another meeting, but as soon as that's over, I'll schedule time on your calendar to work through this, okay?"

Farouk nodded and waved as they exited the elevator and walked in opposite directions to their offices.

By Wednesday, the two had worked through Darren's separation agreement and Lisa's retention offer and gotten Michael's sign-off on both. Michael and Oscar each met individually with select members of the executive team to explain what was happening and how they'd be communicating it to Darren's direct reports and the rest of the organization.

Oscar scheduled back-to-back meetings with Darren and Lisa for Friday morning. Oscar got right to it when Darren arrived at his office, and they were both seated.

"I wanted to follow up with our last conversation about Lisa and Project One," Oscar began. "First, I want you to know that I understand and appreciate how difficult change can be. It also is not lost on me how significant your contributions to ABC have been during your 25-year tenure. With that said, we are committing to a different strategic direction for the company. And we believe that direction is not only critical to our ability to be competitive, but to our ability to stay in business, as well. You know that Michael, the executive team, and I have consistently reinforced the importance of Project One. We need everyone, especially our top leaders, to embrace it."

Darren began rubbing his palms together. He took a deep breath. He could feel Oscar getting closer to what seemed discouragingly inevitable.

Aware of his colleague's body language, Oscar continued, "I left our last discussion with serious concerns. We were clearly at an impasse. As I said, I respect your perspective, but you don't seem open to new information that could help you better understand the difference Project One will make and why that's so important. A critical initiative like this requires flexibility and guidance from our leadership team. Any efforts to actively or passively disrupt it put both the initiative and organization at risk.

"Most importantly, because of your role, you have significant influence over how the entire operations organization perceives and experiences the company's future. For this initiative to succeed, our operations leaders must fully support it. The fact that you're not on board won't stop us from implementing it. So, if you resist or even subtly work against Project One, you won't be happy continuing to lead here.

"I'm sorry, Darren, but based on our last conversation, it is clear to me that getting you aligned so that what we're doing resonates with you will take too much effort, effort that will keep us from moving forward quickly enough. And there is always the possibility that you will never get there. As a result, I think it's best if we part ways," Oscar said.

He handed Darren a folder. "We've prepared a generous severance package."

Darren looked from the folder to Oscar before exclaiming, "Who do you think you are, Oscar? There is no way in hell Michael signed off on this!"

"He did, Darren," Oscar said quietly as he opened the folder to the severance agreement.

"Let me see that," Darren said as he snatched up the papers and skimmed them.

"How long do I have to sign this?" he asked.

"Before I answer that, Darren, I want you to know that I understand you're upset, and probably very surprised by all of this. I don't blame you," Oscar began. "But this isn't a decision that I take lightly. It's also not a decision that Michael takes lightly. You have contributed greatly to where the company is now. No one is questioning that. But to get where we need to go in today's environment, we need to do things differently. And we all must be willing to do the dance that comes along with change.

"I realize it might not feel like it right now, but in the grand scheme of things, this is the best decision for you as well as for the company. You will not be happy here when you continue to resist our changes. And that will create an unpleasant environment for your team members.

"I can see you're angry, and maybe disappointed, and I understand — I've been in your shoes before, too. But I've always landed in a better situation — as have so many of my friends who have been let go. You might not want to hear my advice, but I know from experience that the sooner you put this behind you, the sooner you will see a new set of possibilities.

"To answer your question about the timeline, you'll have 21 days to sign and return the agreement. That gives sufficient time for your lawyer to review it. It's a pretty standard agreement except for the cash payout and restricted stock terms that are more generous than is typical. We tried hard to be fair in how we compensate for the value you've created for the company. Obviously, the terms are confidential."

Oscar paused for a few moments before continuing. "There's a less-typical option that's time-sensitive that I want to talk through, though. We'd like you to consider staying on board as a transition consultant for three months. If you're agreeable, there is also a retention bonus payable at the end of the consulting period."

Eyes flashing, Darren replied, "Are you serious right now? Why would I stay another three months at a place that doesn't want me? Answer that for me!"

Oscar had anticipated this. He'd have the same question if he were in Darren's shoes.

"Darren, I understand you're frustrated," he began. "And I know this isn't easy. We see the consulting offer as a win-win — we'd have access to your institutional knowledge during a critical period, and you'd have even more time to decide what's next for you. I will be flexible and support you no matter what you decide. But we hope you'll accept the short-term consultant offer."

Darren abruptly stood up. "I don't want your support, Oscar. I am happy to leave this company if it doesn't want me here. I'm not going to be a poster child for what happens if you don't support change. Do you have a pen? I'll sign this right now," he said.

"I don't recommend that, Darren," Oscar cautioned. "I do think you should have a lawyer review this first. And you're emotional right now — this isn't the time to make important decisions."

Ignoring Oscar, Darren grabbed a pen from his desk.

"It says I can choose to leave any time in that 21-day

period. Let's make today my last day."

Taken aback by Darren's impulsiveness, Oscar couldn't hide his surprise as he replied, "I respect your decision, Darren. I'll talk with your direct reports and the operations leadership team immediately, then."

"Yeah, you can do that, Oscar!" Darren snapped. "Anything else?"

"I'll have someone from security meet you at your office to walk you out while I deliver your severance agreement to Farouk and let him know today is your last day. He will terminate your access, provide instructions for returning any company property, and send you a photocopy of your signed severance agreement. It's clear you don't have questions about any of this now, but if you do later, you can reach out to me or Farouk directly. I wish you the best, Darren," Oscar said, checking his instinct to reach out for a handshake.

"Thanks. You too," Darren replied sarcastically before storming out.

After Darren blew by her desk, Shannon peeked into the office and asked, "Is everything okay, Oscar?"

"Yeah, everything is fine, Shannon," Oscar answered. "But thanks for checking. Just a tough, but necessary, conversation."

"You know, all the executive assistants talk. And we all believe you are going to make the changes we need — the changes that will help us keep our jobs. You have our support," Shannon encouraged.

"I really appreciate that, Shannon," Oscar said, smiling. "Thank you."

"I have a couple of time-sensitive requests for you," he continued. "Can you have Lisa come up and see me now? And let's schedule a 20-minute priority meeting with Darren's direct reports in my office at 11."

"Will do, Oscar," Shannon replied.

As Shannon exited, Oscar called the head of security to request an escort for Darren. Then he updated Farouk on the meeting and the unexpected outcome. Farouk, who didn't sound surprised, said he had a meeting with Michael in ten minutes and would let him know.

As Oscar hung up, Lisa tapped on the door frame. "Hi, Oscar! What's up?" she asked.

"Hi, Lisa. Thanks for meeting with me on such short notice. Have a seat," Oscar began, grabbing a folded piece of paper from his desk before joining her in the sitting area.

"I owe you a follow-up from our last discussion about you resigning," he continued. "I took everything you shared with me about challenges with Project One and the roadblocks you are facing under serious consideration. I met with Michael and Farouk and offered suggestions on how we should proceed. Here is what I propose."

Oscar unfolded the paper and placed it in front of Lisa. She began reading.

"This looks like an offer letter!" she said, looking up in surprise.

"It is," Oscar replied. "We're hoping we can get you to stay. The letter outlines your new salary, which matches the Old World Bank offer you've already accepted. And, we'd like to offer you additional restricted stock as a longer-term incentive."

Before he could continue, Lisa interrupted Oscar, "This is great, Oscar. And I appreciate it. But like I said, this wasn't about money for me."

"Yes, I understand that, Lisa," Oscar replied. "I heard you loud and clear on some of the challenges with attitudes around Project One. You may have seen the meeting request Shannon just sent you and your peers for later this morning in my office. It's about Darren. Please keep this confidential until then, but Darren is no longer with the company. So, for now, all operations leaders will report directly to me.

"My plan is to evaluate the organizational structure after we've moved through a few implementations. You mentioned being ready for more responsibility. There are no guarantees, but I will seriously consider giving you exactly that as I think about the organizational changes we'll need."

"Wow!" Lisa exclaimed. "I'm completely dumbfounded!"

"Why's that?" Oscar asked.

"Darren has been here forever. His exit is going to send shockwaves throughout the company. Wow! Wow! Wow!" Lisa continued exclaiming.

"I understand," Oscar acknowledged. "When managing change, leaders sometimes have to make tough decisions, especially with something as big as what we're doing with Project One. It starts with getting the right people on board. Otherwise, we will spend most of our energy managing resistance rather than moving forward.

"And, as you can imagine, we have to strike a delicate balance with these changes. We don't want people to be fearful, but at the same time, we want to encourage them to be open to the future and to learning to manage and lead differently. This is where I think your role modeling will be very helpful. If you agree to stay — and I truly hope you do — Diana and I will be leaning heavily on you to provide guidance to not only your credit card customer service leaders, but to all the customer service leaders now that Darren's gone. Are you up for that challenge?" he asked.

"Absolutely, I am! What a surprising way to end this week," Lisa remarked. "Do you need anything from me in advance of the team meeting at 11?"

"No, I'm good. Thanks for asking," Oscar replied. "And I'm thrilled you're staying! Truly! I'll see you back here shortly?"

Lisa nodded and stood to leave. "Oh, before I go, just in case there's any doubt, I accept your offer," she said with a smile.

When the operations leaders gathered in his office later that morning, Oscar shared the news that Darren was no longer with the company. While it wasn't appropriate for him to discuss the circumstances behind Darren's exit, the team rightly assumed that Darren didn't leave by choice. They also knew Darren was resisting the changes.

Oscar gave them a copy of Michael's email that would go out to all staff later that day about Darren pursuing opportunities elsewhere, and that operations leaders would report to Oscar for as long as necessary. Word about Darren's departure was already starting to spread throughout the organization. Many had witnessed Darren's anger as security walked him to the door with his boxed belongings, and others had heard rumors that he called several confidantes, warning them about the direction the company was taking.

Oscar tuned it all out. He knew Darren would have to process his feelings about the company, the situation, and himself. Oscar was always distressed when anyone left a company in anger, but in this case, he was relieved. One of his biggest obstacles — Darren's resistance — was out of the way. And, he was able to retain a key talent, someone who could really help him make things happen.

With Lisa on board, Oscar was ready to roll up his sleeves with Diana and begin making things happen with Project One in a big way.

8
Another Date Night

TRAFFIC WAS LIGHTER than usual for a Friday evening as Oscar dropped off the twins at his in-laws, so he was ahead of schedule when he swung into Antonia's parking lot to pick up the pizza Elena had ordered. The couple loved planning their evening around a robust red wine and the type of spicy pepperoni pie the kids didn't like whenever Elena's parents invited the kids for an end-of-the-week overnight. The meal reminded them of when they fell in love during graduate school at NYU and couldn't afford anything pricier. Back then, though, they would feast on dollar slices and whatever wine was on sale.

Elena had already poured two glasses of Caymus Cabernet by the time Oscar walked in with the warm pizza box.

"Hi, there!" Elena said as Oscar leaned in for a kiss before setting the large box on the kitchen's center island.

"Well, hello to you, too!" he responded with a smile. "Tucker at Antonia's sends his best and says 'hello.'"

Oscar and Elena had been regulars at Antonia's since it opened two years ago.

"Oh, Tucker is so sweet," Elena replied.

With the wine bottle carefully tucked under her arm and the two half-full glasses in her hands, Elena led the way to the dining room. Oscar followed with plates and napkins stacked on the pizza box. He lifted the first piping hot slice onto Elena's plate before serving himself and settling in.

They ate while talking about the latest headlines, where they'd go on their next family vacation, and Oscar's job. She knew he hadn't been looking forward to his conversation with Darren that day.

"How did your meeting with Darren go today? Did he understand?" Elena asked near the end of the meal.

Oscar took a bite of pizza and sipped his wine before responding. "You probably remember that I met with our CEO, Michael, and Farouk, the head of HR, on Monday about removing Darren and trying to keep Lisa, right?" he replied.

Elena nodded yes.

"I was surprised that Michael accepted my recommendation. I took that to mean he trusted my leadership, but maybe that also made me unrealistic about how things would unfold with Darren," Oscar said.

"Why? What happened?" his wife asked.

"It just didn't go as well as I expected, but as I said, my expectations were probably a little off. I guess I thought he figured out he wasn't the best person for his job with this kind of change happening, so I didn't think he would be so outraged and surprised. Disappointed? Sure. But openly hostile? No. And I say that while knowing that ABC has never made a decision to remove a leader this way.

"I truly felt bad for him, and I'd like to think that my compassion showed while he was venting, but he was too upset to notice or hear me. He ended the meeting abruptly and decided today would be his last day, so we lost any hope of a smooth transition."

"Oh, wow!" Elena sighed.

"You know, Darren has made a significant contribution to ABC," Oscar continued. "Unfortunately, he just can't see the possibilities for the future. That also means he can't find a way to align himself with the Project One implementation plan. Both obstacles left me with no choice. I didn't enjoy doing this, but we need this change if ABC is going to survive and grow."

"You've made these types of decisions in the past. I'm sensing this time feels different, though. Why is that?" his wife asked.

"You're right," Oscar began. "I have done this plenty of times. In the past, though, we didn't have such a compressed timeline. That meant I had time to try to bring the leader around. When they've resisted or seemed stuck, I've been able to educate and coach, and provide additional support. I've had time to observe whether the person really is getting on board — or isn't. Think of it as a grace period that allows the individual to work through the changes and see if they can get aligned with where we're going — or not. While they're working through it themselves, I'm monitoring their progress, looking for specifics that help me determine if they can make the shift. I think that's a fair way to handle the situation, but in this case, we don't have that time with Darren. The situation is too urgent and his role and influence are too big."

"I see," Elena acknowledged. "But what other information would you have needed to make the decision to let him go?"

A perplexed Oscar asked, "What do you mean?"

"In the time you've been there, you've drawn some pretty profound conclusions about the culture and why the organization is where it is," Elena explained. "You already understand the company needs something different. You are also a heart-centered, intuitive leader. Why does it feel like you wish you had more data before you decided Darren had to go?"

Oscar wasn't sure how to answer.

"There is no doubt you are a highly authentic leader,

honey," Elena continued when Oscar didn't respond. "But even highly authentic leaders must balance what's in their heart with what's in their head. Clearly, you used the analytical part of your brain when making this decision. I'm wondering if, while you felt certain you made the right decision about Darren, when he disagreed, you might have wondered just a bit if he was right and you were wrong. I wonder if it's his reaction, and your inability to connect with him in that difficult moment, that are sitting with you right now because you're also so heart-centered. Maybe you've absorbed some of what he was feeling," she said.

"Hmmm. There could be something there," Oscar acknowledged before refilling their wine glasses. "It was definitely a much more emotional meeting than I expected, considering how our previous conversations have gone. I mean, it was pretty clear what we needed from him and what he was willing to give us.

"Still, at the end of the day, you never know exactly how people will respond in these situations. Like I said, Darren has done a lot of good things for ABC. I've seen how a leader's self-esteem and identity get intertwined with their roles, and that might be part of what's happening here. With time, in a situation like this, most realize they're more than their job titles and bounce back. That, in turn, often leads them to a better situation or role, one where they're more aligned with the goals, or the process, or the organization. Hopefully, Darren gets there," Oscar said thoughtfully.

Elena reached across the table and squeezed her husband's forearm.

"I understand your concern for Darren. You are such a compassionate man! In case it helps, I'll throw some of your own guidance back at you. You've taught me a lot about change over the past few years. In fact, believe it or not, I use some of your approaches at work on a day-to-day basis," Elena said.

Oscar raised his eyebrows as she continued. "One of the things you've shared with me and I've seen play out over and over again is how your awareness, acceptance, and assimilation phases are universal when it comes to change. That means Darren is going to have to go through his own journey through those phases. And that's not a journey you can take with him. He will have to get to a place where he can accept his new reality, and that could take time — time you don't have, as you've already said.

"Once he does that, he will be able to assimilate into that new reality," Elena said. "It reminds me of that quote by Mark Nepo, the poet: 'We are either broken open or willfully shed.' In this scenario, I'm guessing Darren feels 'broken open' because he believes something is happening to him. He would rather be in a situation where he's the one making a choice."

Oscar smiled before saying, "You are so wise. And you're right; I do understand this. I think the past few weeks have just been emotionally taxing on a lot of levels. I was really nervous about Monday's meeting with Michael and Farouk. That was not only because my recommendation to remove Darren was the antithesis of ABC's culture, but also because, as the new guy, I needed to communicate that I realized that what I was proposing was counter to the company's norm. I didn't want them to think I was advocating for a key personnel change just to make my mark there.

"I also know that some CEOs just aren't ready to take the kind of courageous step I was advocating for. When a bold move goes against the culture, it can easily isolate the leader making the recommendation. In this case, that's me. And Michael might ask himself if I fit into the culture. At the same time, if you really want to change that culture, you have to take action that is markedly different."

Elena jumped in. "Let me ask a question, Oscar. How has Darren's departure been received so far? Have you heard or seen anything yet?"

"Well, it's still pretty early, but I *am* seeing a few signs already," Oscar said thoughtfully. "I heard through the grapevine that Darren has already talked to some in his network here. And I spoke with his direct reports about the situation and explained they would be reporting to me in the interim. They were clearly surprised, but on the other hand, they really seem aligned with where we are headed.

"Once people get over the shock, I think this change will give Diana, Lisa, and me an opportunity to lead by example and demonstrate leadership behaviors we believe are necessary for ABC to have a prosperous future," he said.

Oscar bit into his pizza before adding, "I do expect there will be louder rumblings throughout the organization on Monday, though. Darren has been with us for 25 years. He's well-liked and very knowledgeable. The difficult part about the situation is that we'll have to figure out how to encourage leaders to lean into this new way of operating without creating fear about differing points of view. I don't want people to be afraid that, if they don't agree with me or any of my team, they will lose their jobs. That's not my intention, and it's not what happened.

"But people will form their own narratives regardless of the facts. So we'll continue to monitor where people are. That will require extra effort on my part, for sure, but the result will be amazing if we get the right people on board with the plan. Getting this right will not only create the foundation we need to successfully implement Project One, it will help start to change the corporate culture," Oscar said.

"So, now that you're through this tough week, what's next?" Elena asked.

"The rubber will really hit the road starting next week. The good news is that they've already been working on Project One for two years, and that gives us a head start we aren't going to throw away. We need to redesign some processes; Diana will lead that effort with some of the key stakeholders. I'm pretty sure Lisa is going to stay as head of credit card customer service operations, which is where we're starting. She is highly engaged — a big plus!

"This entire next phase is all about understanding the different stakeholder perspectives and designing a future that integrates those viewpoints. Everybody can't have everything they want because we are limited by costs and timelines, so it will sometimes feel like there are winners and losers. That's an unfortunate reality. Even so, our goal is to create alignment around our work's purpose. That's much bigger than an individual leader's 'wants' — it's about what's best for the organization," Oscar explained.

"So, for many leaders, the most difficult part of this next phase will be letting go of some of what they want for their area. It's up to us running the project to communicate how important it is that we collectively put the mission of the larger organization ahead of egos. Unfortunately, this is hampered by our rewards and incentive systems, which tend to be geared more towards individual performance. That's something I want to talk to Michael and Farouk about," he added.

Elena laughed.

"What's so funny?" Oscar asked, surprised.

"You said the goal is what's best for the organization, and that's bigger than any individual leader," Elena said.

"Yeah," Oscar acknowledged, still not understanding.

"Well, regardless of the reason, that's the same premise behind your decision to let Darren go," Elena replied. "For some reason, you seem to be torn with that decision, yet you're speaking so nonchalantly about the role of the 'greater good' in the next phase of the project. Maybe there is something there for you to look at."

"Hmmm, I can see what you're getting at," Oscar conceded.

Elena finished the last of her pizza before standing up and looking Oscar in the eye. "Regardless of what happens, I love you. There are no right or wrong decisions, and I'm here to support you. I'm confident you'll get the company to where it needs to be. You've already made tremendous progress, and I hope you can see that for yourself," she said before leaning over and kissing her husband on the cheek.

As Elena cleared the table, Oscar sat quietly thinking about the past week and some of the insights Elena had just offered. Deep down, he knew letting Darren go and working to keep Lisa were the right decisions. And he was optimistic about his team's ability to successfully implement Project One. Still, he was almost haunted by Darren's response earlier in the day. This wasn't the time to dwell on that, though. He would deal with it later. Tonight, he needed to channel his competitive spirit into game night with longtime close friends who were just as competitive.

As Oscar walked to the kitchen with his empty wine glass, he knew he was ready to leave the week behind and enjoy a fun evening with comfortable conversation, laughs, and maybe a victory or two.

9

How We See the World

THE FOLLOWING WEEK was quieter than Oscar expected. While he didn't hear many rumblings about Darren's abrupt departure, he knew people might feel a bit rocked. So, he kept his ears open and checked in on customer service organization leaders frequently to gauge the collective sentiment. His instincts told him removing Darren was in ABC's best interest, and slowly, he began to feel more at peace as his rational mind began to understand that as well.

At the same time, with Lisa staying on with a broader leadership role for Project One, Diana became more confident seemingly overnight. During the project's next phase, Diana worked closely over several days with Lisa, customer service leaders, subject matter experts, and other key stakeholders to document current processes and design future-state processes. Following Oscar's change management framework, she needed to uncover different perspectives amongst the project team.

Diana had never done this before, so Oscar joined the first session to observe, provide guidance, and offer support.

After welcoming the group to the first-of-its-kind meeting at ABC, Diana checked her list to make sure she had 100% attendance at the important session. The roster was heavy with leaders and subject matter experts from

Lisa's operations teams, while some key stakeholders, such as compliance, were represented by one person.

Happy to see that everyone was there, Diana began.

"When we restarted Project One, I walked you through our change management framework's three phases: awareness, acceptance, and assimilation. We have done a lot of work up front to ensure people are aware of our work and its importance. I'm happy to say we've created a strong sense of alignment across the organization. This meeting is our first step in moving from the awareness phase into the next one, acceptance. Oscar is here today to support us as we make this transition. Then, I'm kicking him out!" Diana joked.

"I am going to introduce a new design approach for creating our technology requirements. The goal over the next few days is to document our individual and collective understanding of the existing customer service processes from our respective places in the organization. You've already received a list of key processes for Lisa's operations in the order that Lisa and her team need to review them. The first is customer information updates," she explained.

"Is there a reason we're starting with that process first?" Oscar asked, though he already knew the answer. He had met with Diana and Lisa earlier to discuss how to facilitate this next phase with the team.

Lisa promptly responded, "Yes, Oscar, there are a few reasons. First, we get more customer information update inquiries than anything else. We see opportunities for using the new technology to move more of these interactions to self-service. Second, as you can imagine, that will give us significant cost savings. Third, some of the requests require submitting paperwork, which leads to manual processes where mistakes are more likely to happen. So, our goal is to automate some of the back-office work. This is a relatively low-risk, high-reward situation, which makes it a good starting point."

"Makes sense," Oscar replied, smiling. He wanted the group to understand why Lisa was starting there and that he supported her decision.

When Oscar had no other questions, Diana picked up where she had left off.

"Developing process maps will help us better understand each other's knowledge base. If you aren't familiar, think of this type of map as a process visualization. A process re-engineering team member will work with functional stakeholder groups to develop your current-state process maps.

"Once you map a process, we'll come back together so each of you can share the map you've created. This will help all of us see and understand your perspective and any pain points. As we talk, we'll all better understand all the nuances and complexities of the current process. From that new understanding, we will collaborate to develop an integrated process map that includes everyone's input. Then we'll work together to design a new and improved process that addresses the gaps identified by all stakeholders. Any questions?"

As Diana looked around the room, she noticed that several glanced at Oscar, perhaps looking for signs that he approved. Not sure how to read the silence, Oscar decided to address why this exercise was important.

"Diana, do you mind if I offer some additional insight?" he asked.

"Of course not," she replied.

"Since this is a new approach for us at ABC, I want to encourage everyone to speak up if you have any questions or are unsure of something. Everyone here is an equal contributor, regardless of title or role in the organization. And your input is valuable. My role in this is as your team advisor. I'm working closely with Diana and Lisa to make sure we're clear about how we can execute this change framework. If something isn't working as expected, we'll pivot and make modifications. But I'm confident this framework is successful because I've used it in all the organizations I have worked with in the past ten years.

"I'll add that this phase, acceptance, is the most difficult one. Think about how challenging it can sometimes be to appreciate and accept different viewpoints of the world in everyday life. We see differences in politics and in our homes. The workplace is no exception. The inability to appreciate or understand someone else's perspective is the root of a lot of conflict. We want to become aware of those differences so that we can work through them with compassion, align our collective interests, and determine our path to the future," Oscar said.

He looked around the room as he continued. "Individually mapping the current state, then sharing that with the group, will allow everyone to understand your view of the world, if you will. There is no right or wrong with this. It's all about becoming aware of each stakeholder's understanding, having meaningful discussions, and co-creating a solution that's in the company's best interest. If everyone is open to the process and willing to follow our approach, we will end up exactly where we need to be."

Although no one spoke, Oscar could feel the mood lighten. He smiled and nodded at Diana to continue.

She gave each stakeholder group a breakout room and an hour to work with their process re-engineering expert to document in a process map their understanding of the customer information updating process. While the groups worked, Diana, Lisa, and Oscar discussed the session so far and next steps.

"Oscar, when you've done this exercise in the past, what types of responses have you seen?" Lisa asked.

"Great question," he replied. "First, I've found that

people's understandings tend to be very, and I mean very, different."

"What do you mean?" Diana said.

"Well, think about the functional areas represented here. We have people from finance, risk, compliance, operations, technology, and a few other relevant departments. Besides Lisa's team in operations, how many truly know what our employees have to do to update customer information? And what about the process from a customer's viewpoint? There are probably only a few people in the organization who fully understand the details.

"Our support partners, unless they've worked in customer service, probably have a very limited view. At the same time, Lisa's operations team members may have a limited understanding of compliance or regulatory requirements around customer data. What I've seen happen is everyone has parts of the whole, but very few understand most processes in their entirety, especially when a process spans multiple functions. This exercise helps to draw that out so we can create a more comprehensive view of the end-to-end process.

"That's the primary benefit," Oscar pointed out as he reached for his coffee. "In addition, when running projects like this, there are a lot of personalities. Sometimes the loudest voice, or the person with the most authority, might have the narrowest view of what is actually happening. And that can be a problem.

"At the last company I worked for, the risk management team's conservative attitude had a lot of weight in the organization's decisions. People would comment that 'risk always says no' to new ways of doing things. As a result, the culture generally lacked innovation because the modus operandi was to eliminate risk. No level of risk was acceptable.

"However, when we implemented this process-mapping approach and created a way to learn how each stakeholder viewed it, we had robust discussions and, ultimately, an appreciation for how everyone, including risk management, saw things. We designed solutions that balanced risk, costs, and the customer and employee experiences. With the additional information this process provided, everyone began to shift their understanding a bit. That included seeing that risk managers weren't the bad guys. We got people out of their silos, broke down a lot of barriers across teams, and delivered positive outcomes for the business. Having all key stakeholders engaged from inception was critical as we experienced the change journey together," Oscar added.

"How did you manage the differences?" asked Diana.

"The most important thing you can do is ensure everyone has a voice and is heard," Oscar continued. "You'll have to master facilitating those conversations. But practicing compassion is probably the most important skill you can bring to the party, Diana. Hearing the stakeholder's thoughts, empathizing with their pain points, and guiding the team towards the solution that is for the greatest good is the secret sauce. The customer and employee experience are our priority. Everything else flows from there.

"It takes some time to develop the muscle to guide the team there," he pointed out. "The key to getting collective acceptance is helping each stakeholder accept what you're addressing personally first. Remember, these processes become deeply personal to employees, especially since we measure their performance based on how well they execute them. And their compensation and livelihood are tied to how well they do that, right? So, disrupting their routine during a change process can bring up a lot of emotions," Oscar explained.

"I can see how people can become very attached to how they perform parts of their jobs," Diana said.

"Yes, I've seen that within my teams," Lisa observed. "About half of our customer service advisors have been with ABC for more than 25 years. This is all they've known. And despite their longevity, they don't understand what happens in the system outside their piece of it. That's part of why they resist change — they don't have the big picture. Another reason, though, is that historically, the company hasn't been good at implementing changes. It's hard to blame them for wanting things to stay the same."

"Well said, Lisa," Diana acknowledged.

Oscar smiled as he said, "These are all things our change management framework will help us to work through as long as the project team and our key stakeholders are open to it. We are off to a good start!"

They worked independently in the large conference room until project team members began rejoining them at the designated time to share what they had outlined. The group's energy was a mixed bag. Some were clearly excited and engaged, while others remained relatively quiet and somewhat withdrawn. Oscar quietly advised Diana to start with those she thought were the most energized.

"Alright, let's restart our session by reviewing the process maps from Lisa's customer service teams," Diana began. "I'd like to hear from the customer-facing team first."

Oscar had told Diana earlier that people who were closest to the process tended to be more energized during this process. That's because they didn't always have an opportunity to document what they did, then recommend improvements. Doing so was an eye-opening experience that left them proud of all they knew and could share with others.

Not surprisingly, then, those farther from the process were typically surprised to discover how little they actually knew. Oscar had seen some come back with one or two steps for a process that required at least 20. The discovery could make them uncomfortable, especially in a group situation like this. It was a humbling experience that left some questioning their own value.

Oscar wanted Diana to understand that each stakeholder's experience provided valuable insights to the entire team. At the same time, that new awareness could backfire if Diana wasn't sensitive to how team members felt. She needed to help them focus on how their individual understanding — whether in-depth or shallow — came together to create a collective or shared understanding. For everyone to buy into that end result required that they trust each other's viewpoints, regardless of how much they knew about the process.

Megan, a customer service supervisor, presented first. She smiled as she walked through each processing step on the screen, beginning with a customer's call to ABC's toll-free number. Her team's process ended when the customer service advisor ended the call or offered to transfer it to another department in certain situations. There were 35 tasks and decision points. Diana asked Lisa and the others in the room whether they thought anything was missing. Those in customer service agreed it represented the customer information update process quite well. Others said little.

"Thank you, Megan. It looks like we're off to a good start," Diana said. "How about we have our support partners go next? Lena, would you mind sharing?"

Lena was the sole representative from risk management. She slowly stood to take her place in front of the room when Oscar jumped in first.

"Before we get to Lena's process map, I want everyone to know that it is totally normal, and expected, even, for key supporting stakeholders like risk management to have a limited view of the processes we want to change. They don't own these processes and are far less involved than some of us, but they have specific expertise that influences how we need to do certain things. Our group job is to apply that expertise to our processes where it's relevant. I share that now because Lena might feel awkward sharing her understanding of the process after Megan, who is deep in the trenches with all of this, did."

Oscar turned to face Lena before he continued. "Now, when we get into hand-offs between groups, like when manual process monitoring must be performed by a risk or compliance team unit, you will have more to contribute. For this stage, though, Lena, I want you and our other support partners here to think through whether this process resonates with you, or whether you feel like something is missing. You can help by building on the foundation that Megan has started.

"And, as we discuss process pain points after hearing from each area, everyone will have a much better understanding of how we all contribute, along with an appreciation for each stakeholder's experience, no matter how large or small their role. Does that make sense?" Oscar asked.

"Yes," everyone said in unison, with some nodding their heads, too.

Lena smiled in relief. "I get it! And you just saved me a ton of embarrassment because I could only think of six tasks!" she said with contagious laughter. More than a few were, like Lena, relieved to hear Oscar's explanation.

His well-timed observation before Lena presented served the group well as each support partner provided their view of the process. Using Megan's map as a baseline, the team created and agreed on a comprehensive view of what they were currently doing. This collective acceptance around a key customer service process was Diana's first big win.

As they wrapped up, Diana and Oscar knew the team's energy had made a positive shift. They were pleased to see stronger connections building between operations teams and support functions as everyone began to understand the differences in their various viewpoints. And, by coming together in this way, they had the opportunity to clarify and shape their individual understandings in a way that led to collective knowledge and appreciation. Oscar, Diana, and Lisa all saw more than a few lightbulbs going off over heads as the conversation continued.

After breaking for lunch, they all regrouped to repeat the exercise with the next step in the customer information update process, the back-office component. After a productive few hours together again, they created process maps for the end-to-end customer information updating process, from customer-facing phone calls to back-office processes.

With the current steps documented, the group was in a good position to identify areas for improvement before working with the technology team to build a better system. Those improvements were on the next day's agenda.

10
Designing the Future

THE NEXT MORNING, still energized by the working sessions the day before, Diana was ready to lead the Project One team as the group began process mapping their desired future state. Diana knew Oscar wouldn't join the team until later because something unexpected came up. When he called to say he'd be late, he warned that designing the future and applying constraints often creates conflict within a diverse group of stakeholders.

In essence, he said, time and cost constraints would be key factors in the functionality the technology team could deliver. Stakeholders with wish list items, he noted, didn't always get exactly what they wanted. Getting them to buy into the solution for the greater good could present challenges. This is where she'd have to rely on her ability to help resolve conflicts, he advised.

Wanting to continue the momentum from yesterday, Diana was enthusiastic as she addressed the team at the start of their session.

"I think we had a very productive day yesterday," Diana began while pulling up the process graphic the team had created. "I appreciate everyone's contribution to process-mapping where we're at now with the customer information update procedures. There are 36 tasks and decision points. Several of the manual tasks are creating pain points. You all have also identified five risks as well as opportunities for us to improve efficiency. Does this feel like a complete representation of where we're at now?"

Diana looked around the room, observing silent nods of confirmation.

"Lisa, are you and your team good with this as well?" Diana asked.

"Yes," Lisa replied with a smile. "We reviewed yesterday's output before we left for the day, and feel this is a good representation of our current customer information update process."

"Excellent!" Diana exclaimed. "Let's now move towards the next step in our design approach, which is to document the future process we want to build and implement. Our goals are to create a process that is as frictionless as possible, reduce pain points, and manage our risks. Like yesterday, it's best that we start with Lisa's customer service team. They can walk us through their thoughts, since they are closest to the work. Again, we'll use their understanding as a baseline before asking all stakeholders to add their input," she said, looking around for reactions.

"Alright, if we're all clear, I'll turn this over to you and your customer service team, Megan, so we can hear your thoughts on the future-state process. Fernando, as one of our process re-engineering experts, would you mind documenting the future-state process map in real time based on their input?"

Sharing his laptop screen on the large projector, Fernando opened the process-mapping software and let Megan know he was ready.

Megan and her colleagues carefully explained their thoughts on how to streamline the process. They have been following fairly antiquated processes for the past several decades, so they were clearly excited about designing something new. When they wrapped up a few hours later, Diana asked for feedback from support stakeholders.

"This is a strong foundation to start from. Do any of you from risk and compliance have anything to add?" Diana asked.

Lena and her compliance counterpart studied the proposed design while considering regulatory requirements. They also evaluated the proposed steps for automating current manual processes.

"I don't think I have anything to add," Lena replied. "I believe this meets all our regulatory requirements related to customer data. And I feel good about how it eliminates manual processes. These are very good solutions."

Feeling good about this first pass, Diana smiled at Lisa. They continued as other stakeholders reviewed the maps and suggested minor changes. Jayson's technology team, though, had strong opinions about the level of effort required to deliver the solution.

Jayson said, "I hate to be the bearer of bad news, but while this is all technically feasible, I don't think we can deliver everything within a reasonable timeline. It would be very expensive."

"What do you mean? How expensive?" finance lead Brian asked quickly.

"Well, I'm not sure exactly," Jayson continued. "But based on our staffing, I think we'd have to bring in additional contractors to help support development, testing, and so on, if we want to stick to our original schedule of delivering something within the next few months."

"How many of these improvements do you think we could deliver based on current staffing, Jayson?" Lisa asked.

"Well, my best guess is that we could give you about half of these. And, because we're a financial services firm, the regulatory and risk requirements probably take priority," he replied.

"I agree with that," said Lena.

Before Lisa even had a chance to respond, people began talking among themselves about what the team should do next. Diana remembered how, historically within ABC, the first sign of conflict was also the first step toward derailment. It was one reason change wasn't easy at the company.

Feeling the focus beginning to shift and recognizing the team had been working steadily for a couple of hours, Diana suggested everyone take a 15-minute break. They'd return to the topic when they came back.

Diana needed the break as much as anyone. She was experiencing "leader PTSD," flashing back to situations when risk and other support partners would say "No" and derail all progress. Diana needed a few moments to regroup and gather her thoughts. She wished Oscar were there to offer support and guidance, too. Her confident energy that carried over from the day before was beginning to wane.

Most of the team talked amongst themselves near the coffee and pastry station just down the hall from their conference room. After their own quick break, Diana and Lisa returned to the room and huddled at the far end of the conference table, discussing how to get the group back on track. A few minutes later, Oscar joined them.

"Thank goodness you're here, Oscar," a slightly frazzled Diana exclaimed. "We really hit a roadblock with the team a few minutes ago, so we took a break. I did my best to keep us moving forward, but I'm not sure exactly how we can regain our momentum."

Oscar smiled reassuringly. "No problem. And I'm sorry I had to leave the two of you to drive this next phase. Michael had something urgent he wanted to discuss with me. Tell me how the session has gone so far."

"Well," Diana began, "we have what we believe is a good future-state design. However, according to the technology team, it would either be very expensive or take a long time to deliver what we envision. You know Brian from finance, right? As soon as he heard 'expensive,' he said costs could be a concern. On the other hand, we all agreed that risk and regulatory requirements are paramount. It felt like the typical ABC playbook: When conflict arises, we grind to a screeching halt."

"I see," Oscar replied.

Diana sighed and asked, "How do we work through these conflicts, Oscar? I'm open to suggestions."

"We introduce new ways of thinking," he said with a smile.

"This entire change process is new for everyone. We have to ask new questions and offer provocative insights that go against the conventional ABC wisdom and get the team to think beyond the barriers. And then, we have to work with everyone as they navigate their own personal change experience," he said.

"Let me ask you both something," he continued. "What do you think technology and finance are primarily concerned about?"

Diana thought for a moment before responding, though the answer seemed obvious. "Effort level," she said.

"Cost, too," Lisa added.

"That's what it sounds like based on what you've told me," Oscar replied. "Let's take it a step further. If you think about the scope, magnitude, and history of Project One, do you think our technology and finance partners have something in common? Could it be true that every stakeholder is feeling something that causes each to resort to old behaviors?"

Puzzled, Diana and Lisa look at each other. They needed more from Oscar.

"Diana, I'm going to pose this question to you," Oscar said. "Do you remember how, on the day you and I met, we discussed the three lenses of authenticity and I introduced the change framework's three phases?"

"Yes, I do," Diana replied.

"I know it was a while ago, but during that discussion, I mentioned there is one thing that diminishes authenticity more than anything else. Do you remember what that is?"

"Ohhh!" Diana exclaimed. "It's fear. Fear always reduces authenticity."

"Correct!" Oscar said, pleased. "Think about the team's experience. They had a very positive new experience yesterday. As they let their guards down and tapped into their own creative energy, they were more authentic. We could see that happening.

"But they still remember how ABC tries to deliver change — and some might even remember how it's happened at other places they've worked. They've also gone through changes in their personal lives. The beliefs formed from those experiences run deep. So, the most obvious, and often the most expressed concern, usually isn't the only reason someone might begin to resist. Most of us just want to get back to equilibrium in situations where we feel resistance," he continued.

"So, old patterns of behavior emerge. Think of it as a coping mechanism. That usually means that one energizing day together doesn't automatically ensure a new way of doing things, especially with projects that have failed before. We have to continue to offer positive reinforcement so that this new way of driving change and collaborating becomes natural for team members. That's when they will truly become more authentic, and we will create new outcomes," Oscar added.

"Keep in mind, this is just my hypothesis because I wasn't here earlier. But I've seen this type of behavior over and over again, so I'm fairly confident about my assessment. With that in mind, let's offer a few new and expansive ways for the team to think about solving problems.

"It's important we don't discount how anyone feels as part of this, though. If someone is struggling to move past their resistance, we need to be compassionate and support them. Our goal is to lead them back to the creative energy they all enjoyed yesterday," he said.

"How do we get them there?" Diana asked.

"I don't want to take away your authority, but do you mind if I kick off this next phase of the meeting? It will be helpful for me to assess where the team is, then start to lead them where we need them to be. I think it will help both of you to see how I do it, rather than me giving you a script. Once we start transitioning back to that creative energy, you can take over again. I just want to help the team get through this initial pass of resistance," Oscar said.

"That sounds good," Diana said, the relief in her voice obvious, while Lisa nodded.

People began returning to the conference room just as Oscar, Diana, and Lisa were finishing up. They all greeted Oscar, who launched into the next phase as everyone settled into their seats.

"I apologize for missing the first portion of our session today," he began. "I understand we have a strong future-state design, but there are concerns about our ability to deliver the solution within a reasonable time and within budget."

"Yes, that's correct," Jayson said quickly.

"I know leadership is laser-focused on the project's cost, so we have to stay within budget," Brian added.

"I understand and I don't disagree with those concerns," Oscar said reassuringly. "Let me ask a few questions, and maybe your answers will start to shift our thinking towards a series of solutions. I think we really thrived when we were in that high creative energy yesterday. Do you all agree?"

Everyone nodded.

Oscar walked to the flip chart in front of the room.

"Let's get back to that space. Okay, let's first talk about what constraints exist. I think about constraints as falling into three groups: Type 1, Type 2, and Type 3."

He drew three columns on the flip chart and wrote those words atop each column before continuing.

FIGURE 9. FLIP CHART COLUMNS

Constraint Types

Type 1	Type 2	Type 3

"Type 1 are constraints that we simply can't remove. Think regulatory requirements. We can't do anything about them, right? Then, there are constraints we can remove, but doing so requires preparation, time, or even money in some cases. These are Type 2 constraints. They might be functional or even behavioral. For example, people who have been executing the processes we use now will be dealing with a great deal of change when we implement the new technology. We will need a robust plan to get them to a point where they're comfortable. Again, those obstacles we can change with effort are Type 2 constraints.

"Lastly, we have Type 3 constraints. These can be easily removed. Think of them as our low-hanging fruit, our quick wins. As we introduce the various constraints, we create iterations of the processes we want until we finally decide what we will implement.

"So, think about what you created this morning as the ideal design. It's our perfect solution in a perfect world. When we overlay constraints, we end up with a new iteration. And as we operate into the future and introduce new changes, we design another iteration because the context has shifted. Maybe a regulation has changed or a new technology is available. This iterative design process continues to go on. Does that concept make sense?" Oscar asked.

"Do you mean the ideal design isn't what actually gets implemented?" Diana pondered aloud.

"Well, it depends," Oscar replied. "Ideal designs typically don't get implemented because we live in a world where constraints always exist."

"Then why ever create an ideal design?" Diana asked.

"The value is in facilitating an exercise that sparks the creative energy in the design team that gets them exploring what's possible. This is all about embracing innovation. Great innovators are constantly challenged to imagine the potential and think beyond constraints. That's where true innovation lives. If we don't swim in the pool of possibilities, we inhibit our ability to transform in a substantial way."

"That makes sense," Diana remarked as others nodded. "Can you show us how to incorporate the different constraints?"

"Absolutely!" Oscar replied with enthusiasm. "Let's start by overlaying our Type I constraints. What regulations do we need to account for with risk and compliance?"

As the risk and compliance team members explained the situation, Oscar wrote their responses in the Type 1 column on the flip chart. After recording all input, he walked through the impact those restraints would have on various steps and decision points in their design. They repeated the process with Type 2 and Type 3 constraints. When they were done, he shifted to discussing their solution design.

FIGURE 10. FLIP CHART COLUMNS WITH FINAL CONSTRAINTS

Constraint Types

Type 1	Type 2	Type 3
• Banking regulations • Anti-money laundering rules • Data privacy laws • Consumer protection regulations	• Culture – changing employee behaviors • Culture – ABC's risk appetite • Project budget • ABC's financial position • Shareholder and market perception • Technical limitations	• ABC's corporate policies and procedures • Project delivery timeline • Prioritization of work • Functional requirements

"Okay, so the big question is: How do these constraints impact our design?" Oscar mused. "The changes we need to make to it have to mitigate our concerns around time and budget. It would be helpful for us to think about value creation. Where do we create the most value in this process? And where do we stand to destroy value? In essence, where can we create a frictionless experience for our customers and employees? And where does it not really matter?"

Lisa sat up straighter before sharing her thoughts.

"Some of our manual processes are necessary because of regulatory requirements. We do them well, and the customer experience is not directly impacted by many of them. They are simply government requirements. So, if there is a significant cost to automate those, I would suggest that we keep the manual processes and focus on something like the self-serve capabilities that will save customers, our employees, and the company time and money," she said.

"Exactly! That's just where I'm going, Lisa," Oscar replied before sipping from his ever-present water bottle. "Not every step in the process facilitates high value creation. I'll add that we should put our energy into changing our design in areas that create critical incidents for customers, complexity for our staff, or excess costs for ABC. This is how we can deliver the most value."

Diana made mental notes about the way Oscar masterfully explained how to move from ideal design to what would eventually be the team's first design iteration. His poise and ability to embrace team members' various perspectives helped them transition back to the highly creative group they were the day before. And in a matter of an hour, everyone regained their enthusiasm about the future processes they wanted to deliver.

After they returned from another break, Diana took over. By the time they were done, they all agreed on the first iteration of the customer information update process. There were certain process steps that would remain manual for the time being. But the team was confident they could automate others that created significant value not only for ABC, but for its customers and employees, as well.

Moreover, Jayson, Brian, and other key stakeholders who had expressed concerns early on were relieved that they were heard and that there were workable solutions. As they did the day before, the team closed the day out feeling good about their progress.

Diana's confidence returned, too. She could see how this new approach helped them deal with institutionalized, unproductive behaviors. The shift happened quickly for some and more gradually for others.

Diana's meeting high wouldn't last too long, though, as Oscar told her and Lisa that he needed to share new information with them that would introduce more complexity to their already complex transformation. The project team wasn't meeting tomorrow, so they agreed to get back together in Oscar's office first thing the next morning.

11

An Unexpected Disruption

DIANA AND LISA arrived together at Oscar's office promptly at 8 a.m. "Good morning," he said with a smile. "I wanted to connect with you first thing to share that update I mentioned. How about taking a seat?"

The women were intrigued by the conflict between the urgency to meet and Oscar's calm demeanor. As she and Lisa each took a seat on the couch in the center of Oscar's office, Diana found herself remembering the first time she had met Oscar there. Then, she had been anxious because she expected to be fired. She had that same nervous feeling in her stomach now.

"Listen, I want to give you a heads-up on some critical new information, and I want to be as transparent as possible," Oscar began as he closed his office door. "First, what I'm about to share is highly confidential, at least for the next few hours. So, I need absolute discretion from both of you."

The women nodded.

Oscar continued, "Yesterday morning, Michael called an emergency meeting of the executive team. That's why I missed the first part of the Project One design session. You both know Michael is well-connected with a few senior government officials. He confided during that session that there will be an announcement later this morning about a highly probable trade war between our government and other nations. My understanding is the impact could be far-reaching and widespread. There is no doubt there will be critical implications to our businesses in the short term, and maybe longer, depending on how all this plays out."

"Whoa. I didn't see that coming so quickly, but I can see how that will create uncertainty across all industries," Diana began. "What are you thinking about with regards to Project One specifically?" Diana asked.

"As you know," Oscar began, "this country has had periods of slow growth and inflation for years. Coupled with challenges in a housing market that has priced many people out, we are at a bit of an economic tipping point. An unexpected disruption with our trade partners could be the catalyst that creates a significant economic downturn. Michael is hearing that directly from a senior economic advisor.

"And if our customers are worse off, demand for our products and services will drop. We can expect substantial revenue decreases across our entire portfolio. I'm not trying to scare you because we have all survived economic downturns in the past. But it's the uncertainty while delivering Project One that is the biggest concern. And that's where there is a direct connection to the three of us.

"We are going to have to lead the organization through what might become a volatile set of circumstances. ABC's current position, which Project One is supposed to fix, puts the company more at risk than our industry peers are," he said.

"Ahhh," Diana sighed aloud. "Well, this seems like it might be a lot to handle."

"Yes, it's very concerning. I can see how this could put us out of business if it doesn't go well," Lisa added.

"In truth," Oscar began again, "there are a lot of unknowns, so anything is possible. It will be all hands on deck, but I see us playing a critical role because of the work we're driving. I'll share more details with you once we have them. For next steps, Michael expects the board to get heavily involved as we figure out the implications for us. Some are saying that the government's position on trade is just a negotiation tactic, so this could be a big nothing burger. But we all know that as new information becomes available, people react. And it doesn't matter whether the information is highly credible or not. In my opinion, knee-jerk reactions are the bigger concern. A highly uncertain environment makes designing strategies very difficult, partly because people are highly distracted by that uncertainty. So, all I can say is let's get ready, and we'll get through this. Questions?"

"Yes. Is there anything we should do differently right now?" Diana asked.

"No, no changes at the moment," Oscar replied with confidence. "We've made good progress with Project One. Let's continue that momentum. We'll talk to the team once the information is public and the executive team has provided guidance. For now, it's business as usual."

"Sounds good," Diana said.

As they left Oscar's office, Diana and Lisa decided to discuss the news further in Diana's office.

"So, that was a bomb, yes?" Lisa asked as she closed Diana's door.

"Yeah, it was! It's almost unbelievable. Just when I thought we were in the clear and things would sail smoothly over the next few months, this happens," Diana replied. "I will say this: There is no one I'd rather have guiding us through this than Oscar. Did you see how calm he was? He didn't overreact. He doesn't seem to be concerned about how this might play out for himself, us, or the organization. I admire how he seems to really go with the flow when he responds to new information. I don't think I've ever seen anyone operate that way before."

"I agree. What will be interesting to see is how he manages all this with *that* executive team. We are seeing old behaviors with some of the Project One people. But imagine having to navigate that with the top leaders in the company who practically *instituted* those behaviors," Lisa mused.

"I have to think Oscar knew he'd have to manage that at some level anyway," Diana replied.

"I guess you're right," Lisa said. "Well, let me get my day started. My group mentioned they like our progress, which is just one way this feels very different than our last go round. Oscar is obviously playing a huge supporting role, but you've done a great job of leading us, Diana. And that's feedback directly from my team! Your leadership is shining. Keep it up!"

Blushing, Diana replied, "Thank you, Lisa. That means a lot coming from you. I've always admired how you lead and hope to follow in your footsteps. And honestly, I'm so glad people are experiencing me differently. I feel like what I've learned and had a chance to implement over the past few months has me feeling much more like myself. I'm feeling a freedom and comfort level that I haven't really had here before. I feel safe. I guess you could say I'm becoming more authentic. Geez, I sound like Oscar, don't I?" she laughed.

Any tension from Oscar's news was gone as Lisa left and Diana began prepping for the next series of Project One design sessions.

Later that morning, as Oscar had predicted, government officials announced more aggressive strategies with trade partners. As the news sent shockwaves throughout the world, financial markets responded unfavorably. Concerns about global consequences and the country's economic future dominated the afternoon news cycle. Before the end of the day, CEO Michael emailed all employees to address the news and state that the leadership team would continue monitoring the situation, but there would be no changes in the organization's operations now.

With Oscar's approval, Diana held an impromptu meeting with the Project One team to discuss why it was important that they stayed focused on their mission despite the unexpected development. Leading by example, Diana made more progress guiding the project design sessions the following week. Everything seemed to be running smoothly despite the global trade situation.

A few weeks later, the administration in Washington created more disruption by changing course. And did that again the following week.

ABC found itself trying to determine an appropriate response to what had become an increasingly and alarmingly fluid environment. Erik, ABC's board chair, called an emergency meeting with the board and executive team to discuss the organization's status and any potential changes in its strategy.

Erik got right to the point. "Michael, would you mind giving the board your executive team's perspective on the potential for what is a highly probable trade war? It's now clear this could trigger a severe economic downturn that impacts our business," he said.

Michael cleared his throat before responding. "We've run a few financial models to get a better sense of the potential impact across our product portfolio, and the outcomes don't look good. We believe the greatest impact will be on our consumer businesses, which are already in a challenging state. As you know, Oscar's Project One is designed to help reposition us in the marketplace. We're implementing it now, but are still about six months away from realizing any material benefit from it. Anything to add, Robert?"

The CFO swirled the coffee in his mug before speaking.

"I'll add that the trade situation's impact on our financial position will lag as consumer sentiment shifts over time. So, not much will change over the next quarter or so, but our models suggest there will be a significant performance drop-off in about six to nine months. That could lead to a situation where we simply cannot recover. If that scenario does indeed play out, my department estimates that we'd have a runway of about 12 to 18 months before we'd have to shut our doors. I'd be kidding you if I didn't say those of us in finance are anxious."

Erik's face became even more serious as he turned to Michael and asked, "Michael, what strategic options have you and your teams been exploring to mitigate this risk?"

"We're considering a few different options," Michael replied quickly. "Let's have everyone on the executive team here update us on their areas."

Oscar leaned forward with interest. He wasn't sure what to expect from his peers since up to this point, most of the executives appeared to be working in silos, not sharing with one another the plans their groups were considering. He suspected that the leaders had brought Michael up to speed, though.

It was a given, Oscar knew, that executive team members wouldn't be aligned. Unfortunately, a set of disjointed strategies at such a high level was business as usual at ABC. Oscar knew that this time, though, the lack of alignment could mean a disastrous future for the company.

Robert spoke first. He noted that his group was focused on exploring additional expense management strategies by cutting costs beyond what was already planned. Bijal, ABC's chief risk officer, expanded on Robert's position by discussing how his group was exploring certain new AI technologies that could help them maintain their required vigilance while reducing staff. Continuing down the expense-cutting path was Farouk, the chief human resources officer. He recommended focusing on reducing staff within centralized functions and reducing corporate overhead. He also suggested they contract with a change management consultant to help them navigate such a large disruption.

Oscar noticed how each leader's strategy was limited to cost-cutting measures. Was that because they had limited strategic perspectives about how to move a business forward in general? Or was it because they were resorting to traditional conservative tactics and behaviors that had kept ABC in business for the past 75 years? Maybe it was a combination of both, he thought. In any case, they seemed to be leading from their separate spaces in the organizational chart rather than looking at ABC holistically.

Phillip, the chief growth officer, broke the monotony by providing an update on a new customer segmentation strategy along with product innovations his team was exploring. Oscar was pleased to hear a strategic insight that looked beyond cost reductions. Chief Technology Officer Lora continued in the same vein, speaking about the importance of maintaining focus on Project One. It would reduce costs, drive customer engagement, and increase revenue, she emphasized. Lora also mentioned a new technology project she was exploring with Phillip that required investment and had a longer delivery timeline.

Erik and the board responded favorably to everything, but especially to what they heard from Phillip and Lora.

"Oscar, would you mind wrapping up with your update?" Erik prompted.

"Sure," Oscar obliged. "In short, we aren't planning to do anything significantly different across operations."

Erik trusted Oscar, so he wasn't thrown by Oscar's response. He calmly asked, "Can you elaborate for us?"

"Of course," Oscar began as he looked around the table.

"Project One has 100% been the most important focus across operations. Before the trade announcements, it was also the most important strategic initiative across ABC. I think we all would agree with that, right?"

As heads nodded, Oscar continued. "Here's what my team and I are thinking. First, pivoting to a new strategy would require taking resources away from Project One, and that initiative remains essential to our future viability. Cannibalizing it would be counterproductive. Second, Project One still creates the most value-add from all the potential opportunities we've explored. Finally, we are much more focused on clarity now, and that allows us to lean into the uncertainty in a different way."

"What do you mean by a focus on clarity?" asked Erik.

"We have no control over the administration's decisions and the implications of its trade announcements. That aside, organizations in general tend to focus on outcome consistency rather than learning to ride the wave. That's not always a good thing," Oscar replied.

Michael looked puzzled.

Oscar cleared his throat before continuing. "As a public company, we are beholden to our shareholders. We offer them a return through stock appreciation and dividends. The price of our stock is impacted by information and our performance against expectations. Most notably, several of us give presentations during the quarterly earnings call so we can share information that helps investors better understand the future outcomes we're projecting.

"Those shareholders value certainty. And the reality is that nothing is certain. So, when things feel uncertain, ABC tends to be quick to take what may be well-designed plans and throw them out the window to appease a set of short-term expectations," he said.

Oscar looked around the conference table as he continued.

"I want everyone to think about this. When you've had powerful moments of clarity, how did you respond to information that might create a level of uncertainty? You all know that when you are clear, you ride the uncertainty in a very different way. There is no fear. No self-preservation. You operate with a strong sense of who you are and what you stand for. You tell others, 'Trust me. This will work.' My team knows Project One is mission critical, so we aren't going to lose sight of that as the world shifts around us."

As several of the people in the room began nodding, Oscar continued. "My team and I are focused on how we ride the wave of uncertainty differently from how it's unfolded at ABC in the past. It's about us navigating the distractions *with clarity*. While the administration in Washington, D.C. has created uncertainty for the majority of organizations like ours in this country by waffling on its trade position, my team has remained laser-focused on what we believe is the best strategy: Project One.

"As part of that, we have created additional communication mechanisms so information flows up to me, then down again to our frontline customer service employees. We've also added more leadership check-ins to make certain that everyone is aligned with the stage we're at on our journey and has adequate information to handle questions and concerns. Leading through this change in this situation is more about how we deal with change than it is about pivoting to a new strategy. Changing strategies would definitely hurt our momentum with Project One," Oscar concluded.

"I think that rationale makes a lot of sense," Erik said, leaning back in his chair at the head of the table.

Michael, although still taken aback by how different Oscar's approach was, saw the value in it. There was nothing for him to critique. But he did have an idea he thought would be a step towards increasing ABC's long-term stability while building favor for him with Erik and the board.

"Oscar, I think that approach is brilliant. Let's talk about incorporating your strategy on an enterprise level at our next executive meeting. We should also use that session to explore some of the other strategies discussed that could run parallel to Project One."

"Sure, I'd be happy to discuss an approach for the company," Oscar agreed.

As he nodded approvingly, Erik brought the emergency meeting to a close. "We have solid potential action steps. I move to immediately create a new board committee that is focused on helping us navigate the uncertainty of the current economic environment. I nominate Oscar to lead that committee with our three independent directors, plus Lora and Farouk as members. Let's plan on reconvening in two weeks."

The board members unanimously approved Erik's suggestion, and the meeting adjourned.

As he returned to his office, Oscar reflected on the experience. He knew he had left a positive impression on nearly everyone, but especially Erik and Michael. From his perspective, this was the perfect time to lean into leading more authentically and begin bringing members of the executive team along with him.

He had become the key to several locks that day. Right now, though, he needed to get back to work with Diana, Lisa, and the Project One team. He knew team members were all processing the economic uncertainty in different ways. To succeed and keep their positive momentum, Oscar needed to ensure that everyone was comfortable riding the wave of uncertainty. He also knew that it was an uphill battle.

12
Getting to Clarity

THE FOLLOWING WEEK, the Project One team had a full agenda that included final testing of the first rollout's new functionality. While the developers worked on that, Diana brought the rest of the team together to begin the next design session series. Oscar knew Diana was comfortable leading the group, but he opted to attend the first meeting in case there was chatter about the emergency board meeting and ABC's response plans. The team had gained significant momentum in a short period of time, and he wanted to make sure that concerns about outside circumstances didn't derail that progress.

Diana was grateful he was there as participants arrived in the conference room with a collective mood that didn't match a typical Monday morning meeting. People usually arrived at start-of-the-week meetings talking about their weekends or enjoying light banter. Today, there was near silence.

"Good morning! I hope everyone had a great weekend. Seems like the energy here is a bit low this morning, though. Is everything okay?" she asked.

Nobody spoke. And Oscar knew why. He decided to address it head-on.

"You all know this is a safe space. And I have a couple guesses about what's going on here," Oscar said. "Who wants to be the first to talk about what's on your minds?"

Jayson made eye contact with Oscar but remained quiet.

"Jayson?" Oscar probed.

"Well, I heard there was an emergency board meeting late last week to discuss the government's position on global trade. And based on what people are saying about the potential impact, ABC won't fare too well," Jayson said.

"Right. Thanks for getting us started, Jayson," Oscar replied. "Anything else?"

"That's the gist of what I heard, and I'm sure everyone else here heard it, too," Jayson added.

Oscar smiled reassuringly as he replied, "Early in my career, I worked with a leader who, at his monthly town halls, never failed to ask everyone there if they'd heard any good rumors lately. So, I throw that question out to all of you now. I imagine most of you are aware of the emergency board meeting Jayson mentioned, which did indeed take place late last week. What rumors are swirling because of that?" Oscar asked the room.

After a few seconds of silence, Lena chimed in. "I heard we are getting rid of the risk management department and need to cut 30% of all staff, or we will be out of business within a year."

That opened the floodgates.

"I heard that we are going to stop working on Project One and stick with our old systems," Megan added.

Fernando piled on, "I heard our CEO is going to be fired unless he develops a new strategy for the company, but he's choosing to resign instead. That means we'll soon be looking for his replacement, and that bothers me. I like Michael."

"I've heard some version of everything that's been shared thus far," Lisa added.

"Me too, Oscar," Diana said.

"So, based on what you all heard, how do you feel about

it?" Oscar asked.

"I don't want to speak for the group," Brian began, "but none of this feels good. And I feel like I should probably start looking for another job if I'm being totally honest. Seems like ABC will soon be dead in the water."

Oscar couldn't ignore the chorus of "Yeahs" around the table as he continued probing. "I hear you," he said. "How did this information impact your weekend or your day-to-day work?"

Someone said loud and clear, "My weekend sucked!"

Another said, "I haven't been able to focus on my job."

Oscar knew it was time for him to infuse the space with his signature calming energy, so he stood up and began walking around the room while speaking.

"Let me start by saying that I empathize with all of you," he said. "In fact, I empathize with people who have no connection to ABC because if this new trade strategy happens as stated, it will have a global impact not just on businesses, but on citizens everywhere. Let me give you some context about the meeting and share what happened and the potential ramifications for us.

"The board wanted to hear the executive team's plans for handling the impending trade war's impact on the company. I'll be honest. When Michael and Robert, our CFO, presented various financial models, they did indeed include a scenario where ABC could be out of business. That shouldn't be a surprise to you, though, because you all know that we're designing and implementing Project One to avoid that exact scenario, regardless of any changes in trade policies. Admittedly, this unexpected potential for an economic downturn could speed up that demise if we don't do our jobs with Project One.

"Each executive presented actions their functional areas could take to improve our positioning. As you would expect, several — but not all — discussed cost cutting.

But some talked about other options, including product expansion. This is important for you to know, because it wasn't all doom and gloom. The overarching theme was that we need to figure out what we want to do as a business. That implies some level of change, right?" Oscar asked as he looked around the table before continuing.

"This gave me a pivotal opportunity to reinforce Project One's importance to our entire organizational health. I explained that taking resources away from us to save money would be detrimental, regardless of what happens economically. Instead, we need to focus on managing the distractions because the trade situation we have no control over seems to be changing daily. We will get much better outcomes if we stay focused on our mission and work toward clarity rather than using certainty as our goal.

"Uncertainty is everywhere, and it often sparks fear," Oscar continued. "We can't control what the administration is going to do or how people will react. But we *can* control how we respond to it, and a big part of the way all of us steer this ship is by learning how to ride the waves differently.

"I hope you can see that this is an incredible leadership opportunity for all of you," Oscar continued. "My role is to support you as we navigate this together. I'll offer clarity when I can. And clarity doesn't mean I will have all the answers. I won't, because I'll be riding the waves right along with you. But I will be transparent about what is known and unknown. We have to somehow find our way to being comfortable with that. Otherwise, we will easily be consumed by every new bit of information that shows up.

"Most of us crave certainty because of some underlying fear. I believe leaning into clarity is much more important than certainty. When you are clear about who you are, you don't have to fear the unknown. You stand in your power differently. Let me illustrate this by using one of you as an example. How about you, Lisa?" Oscar asked.

Lisa didn't know where Oscar was headed, but she agreed to be the guinea pig for this exercise anyway.

"Okaaay," she said, both nervous and curious.

"If ABC went out of business tomorrow, Lisa, what would you do?" Oscar asked.

Surprised by the question, Lisa was quiet for a few seconds before saying, "Honestly, I don't know. Maybe I should have, but I haven't really given it much thought, to be honest," she replied.

"Let me ask a different question," Oscar continued. "Have you ever thought about leaving ABC?"

Lisa was taken aback by the question. Oscar knew she had turned down a competitor's offer recently, so why was he asking this, and why was he forcing her to admit in front of her team that the answer was yes?

"Yes, I've thought about it," Lisa answered hesitantly. But she trusted Oscar, so she continued to engage in his impromptu experiment.

"What are some of the factors you considered then?" Oscar asked.

"I thought about things like how much time I've spent at ABC and the relationships I've developed here," Lisa began. "I factored in compensation, what's involved with learning a new organization, and whether they support hybrid workplaces. I know that several of our competitors now require staff to work in the office every day, and that doesn't appeal to me, especially on Fridays. With our flexibility, I can start my weekend with my family sooner than if I had to commute home from an office. Did I want to give that up?"

"I get it," said Oscar. "Let's go a little deeper now. When you were thinking about your career options, how did you feel about ABC at the time? And how did you feel about the possibility of starting at another organization?"

Lisa, remembering the not-so-distant past, fiddled with her pen before replying. "I won't get into the details, but to be honest, I was very upset about how things were playing out at ABC. I didn't feel valued."

"Is it fair to say you were experiencing resistance while at ABC, and so you decided to explore other options?" Oscar asked.

Knowing full well about Lisa's recent decision to leave — and then stay at — ABC, Diana knew exactly where Oscar was heading.

"Yes," Lisa acknowledged. "And it didn't feel good at all."

"That's right," Oscar confirmed. "Resistance doesn't feel good for most of us. And for many, our default behavior is to find a way to quickly move from resistance to resonance, or a place of alignment, that feels better. That is a very natural response. In your situation, you chose to get that resonance by exploring employment elsewhere. But you're still here with us at ABC, you're smiling, and we're very happy you are here!"

Everyone laughed as the tension left Lisa's shoulders and she smiled.

But Oscar wasn't done. "Depending on how long ago you had this inflection point, my guess is that somewhere along the decision-making path that led you to staying here, you found resonance with your ABC situation. Something changed. Otherwise, you'd still be feeling resistance. And we wouldn't be experiencing the level of joy and passion you show up with every day. Those are symptoms of resonance, not resistance. Is that a fair assessment?"

"Absolutely," Lisa smiled.

"Here is the point I want to drive home," Oscar continued. "This is all about how we move from resistance to resonance and vice versa. It's a constant balancing act as we experience different facets of life. However, the most important aspect of all this is recognizing that we have the power to choose. And though relief might not come instantaneously, we make decisions that lead us to a place of resonance if we're trying to find relief. In your example, Lisa, you made the choice to explore alternative opportunities. I'm sure that felt empowering. I often refer to a great line from a book by poet Mark Nepo that says something like, 'We are either broken open, or willfully shed.'

"This is such a powerful thought," Oscar said as he looked around the table. "Lisa's conscious decision to choose is like willfully shedding. Many of us feel powerful when we decide what we want to do instead of waiting for some*one* or some*thing* to decide *for* us. On the flip side, something like ABC going out of business — which means the decision is taken from you — is the equivalent of Nepo's broken open. And when you are broken open, it's very easy to feel like you've lost your power because, in this case, you didn't choose to change jobs. However, if we learn to navigate the heavy emotions that may come with being broken open, we can choose what we want to do in response. Then we regain our sense of power.

"For many people, the most expansive moments of growth happen when they are faced with something very difficult. That often forces us to look deeper within. However, if you get stuck focusing on getting back to resonance as soon as possible, you don't always see that you still have the power to choose. Many of us give up our power when bad things happen to us. And we struggle with emotions like fear, doubt, shame, and so on," Oscar said.

"I share all this to say that you are powerful, whether you feel like you are willfully shedding or you're broken open. It's all a series of choices. And if we understand that life will throw things at us that we both do and don't want, we can hold onto our power. Ultimately, we learn to ride the waves differently.

"I've been broken open in unexpected ways throughout my career and in my personal life, too. But when I put those experiences into proper perspective, each has been a catalyst for transformational growth. It's kind of like what Kelly Clarkson sings — what doesn't kill us makes us stronger, right? And I'm deeply grateful for all those often unpleasant experiences because they have shaped who you see in front of you today."

As she watched Oscar's words alter the room's dynamic, Lisa crossed her arms over her chest and leaned back in admiration before catching Diana's eye and smiling. Others smiled, too, as their collective anxiety dissipated. Oscar was speaking truth to power, and everyone could feel it.

"With all that said, let's get back to everyone's immediate concern," Oscar began again. "The board wants me to lead a committee that develops an enterprise approach to how we navigate these times. My guess, and it's only a guess, is that the committee will consult on any strategy changes. For right now, though, that isn't the focus. We haven't made any decisions about costs, new products, or anything else. We're having another board meeting in a few weeks. And I'm sure that will generate new actions based on the latest information. My commitment to you is that I will keep you informed of what's coming. You will always get the truth from me. So, does all that help?" he said as he looked around the table and smiled.

He didn't hear a single "no."

"Oscar, should we consider any changes for Project One?" Diana asked.

"Not right now," Oscar quickly replied. "This project is still the most important strategic initiative at the company. And I know our delivery speed will pick up as we go through additional design sessions and everyone feels more comfortable with our change framework.

"This team is doing a great job! My only suggestion is that if you can focus even more on Project One, now would be the time to lean in. The organization is counting on you," Oscar replied.

With their immediate concerns addressed, Diana led her team through another productive design session that lasted the rest of the day. As the group filed out, talking about their next steps, Anastasia, the group's HR representative, approached Oscar.

"Oscar, could we talk for a moment?" she asked.

"Of course, Anastasia. What's on your mind?" Oscar asked.

"I wanted to share with you how much your resistance and resonance examples hit home with me. I've had a few of those broken-open experiences that really changed me at my core," she explained.

"I'm glad you connected with the message," Oscar replied. "Should we sit?" he asked, motioning to two chairs recently vacated as the room emptied.

They sat as Anastasia recounted how she came to ABC.

"My husband and I tried to have a child for a very long time," she began. "When we finally conceived, we were blessed with a beautiful baby girl we named Jasmine. To say we were ecstatic is an understatement. Our joy didn't last long, though, because when Jasmine was just four months old, we learned she had a rare and aggressive form of pediatric cancer. We lost her just before her first birthday."

"Oh, wow! I had no idea. I'm so sorry," Oscar said as he touched her arm.

"Thank you. I appreciate your compassion. And we are doing okay," Anastasia said. "As you can imagine, I was fairly emotional. I was angry, fearful, sad, and any other dark emotion you can think of. I went into a deep depression that impacted my home and work lives. Every day, I felt that resistance you've defined and described for us.

"After spending time in therapy and doing a lot of self-work, I eventually found my way to acceptance, which put me in a better place. After that, I began to feel grateful, surprisingly enough, because I realized Jasmine was a catalyst for giving and receiving unconditional love in a way I didn't think was even possible. My husband and I started connecting differently as we learned to honor the gift of this shared experience. We both found our way to feeling more aligned with life again — less like we were outside looking in and more like we were participants.

"And, we began volunteering at our local children's hospital, working with families of children with cancer. We found a sense of purpose as a light for people experiencing some of their darkest times," she explained.

"That's amazing, Anastasia. I admire your newfound strength and how you're using it to help others," Oscar said with compassion in his voice.

"Honestly, if that experience hadn't happened, I probably would've never come to ABC," Anastasia replied.

"Oh, really? How is that?" Oscar asked.

"When I told my story at a hospital fundraiser a few years ago, Farouk was in the audience. When he singled me out for a conversation afterwards, I mentioned that I worked in HR. Turns out he was looking for a new senior leader for his HR team, so he asked me to consider joining him at ABC. The rest is history, as they say. I'm really enjoying working here, so I'm glad we had that serendipitous encounter. And your approach to change management leaves me feeling enthusiastic about where we're headed and how we'll get there."

"I appreciate you sharing your remarkable story, Anastasia, and I'm glad this experience is having a positive impact on you," Oscar remarked.

"Can I ask you a question?" Anastasia said hesitantly.

Oscar nodded.

"What has made you so interested in and good at change management?" she asked.

"Well, a lot of things," Oscar began. "But there are probably a few key experiences that really pushed me onto this path. Early in my financial services career, I had a handful of mentors who provided something of a leadership playbook. They helped me see that both education and experience were required if I wanted to have a senior leadership role in the industry. I followed their advice while building a strong network, too. And I was rewarded with a speedy move up the ladder, so to speak.

"However, because I invested so much of my energy into my career, my personal life suffered. I was chasing titles, money, power, influence — you know the drill. I know you've seen it in others. I wanted all the things that came with my definition of success. But the journey there was increasingly painful. After a mental health incident that led me to a therapist, I realized that deep down, I wasn't very happy.

"Around that same time, my good friend Joe encouraged me to vacation with him in Turks and Caicos. I'm glad I accepted the invitation because that time away came at just the right moment. It allowed me the space I needed to just relax and decompress.

"On the second day, we walked silently along the beach in the morning, enjoying the sounds of waves hitting the shore while the sun warmed us. It was positively cathartic — and exactly what I needed. As we stopped to watch the water's movement, at some point, Joe's eyes seemed fixed on something in the distance, so I asked what he was staring at."

Oscar smiled at Anastasia before continuing.

" 'See that incoming current over there?' Joe asked, pointing to the motion going diagonally from left to right.

" 'Now, over there?' he asked again, pointing to another incoming current moving diagonally the opposite way, from right to left.

" 'Watch these two currents come together. They just merge and create a new current. It's amazing how much nature teaches us,'" he said.

"I didn't understand what he meant," Oscar continued, "until Joe explained how nature is always either in flow or resonance. There is no resistance. If you think about the two currents as human perspectives, we can either integrate those perspectives and create something new that offers resonance, or we can hold fast to our perspective. Doing that is like the currents continuing to push in their original direction. When they meet, they resist each other. When people do this, there's no flow, no flexibility.

"There is so much wisdom in this, isn't there?" he asked Anastasia. "I was surrounded by nature so often on that vacation. I walked the beaches and hiked through forests. I was fascinated by the frequent weather shifts — clouds would roll through with rain in the morning, and 20 minutes later, we had clear skies and sunshine. Sometimes I just stretched out on the beach and looked up at the sky. As I did that, I realized how it's always changing. Clouds are constantly shifting, never to repeat a formation. The sun shows up, then disappears behind a cloud.

"It brought home something I had never noticed before because my focus was always elsewhere. I realized that nature in general is always changing. As humans, though, we often want things to remain the same. Change, in essence, is against our nature — even though change is constant in the natural world. As a result, we experience resistance," Oscar explained.

"Once this understanding really sank in, it changed how

I think about how I can lead. The individuals who populate businesses are constantly changing. The outside world is constantly changing. The best way to navigate that ever-present change, in my opinion, is to embrace it. To do that well, you need leaders and employees who also accept and appreciate change. When people who value change come together, they create an organization that is stronger and more resilient. We can do that here at ABC."

"That's an amazing story, Oscar, and more metaphysical than I expected from you!" Anastasia remarked. "I guess Diana's Project One design sessions are like the currents in the ocean, right? Her job is to help merge us together rather than having one current insist on pushing in a particular direction."

"You've got it!" Oscar exclaimed, high-fiving her. "That's why it's important that people are heard during that process. They need to feel safe enough to reveal their ideas and concerns. This is how the process increases authenticity. And that momentum just builds as participants return to their day jobs and lead in a way that resonates with who they truly are."

"Hmmm," Anastasia sighed. "That's pretty brilliant."

"I don't know if it's brilliant," Oscar laughed, "but what I *do* know is that it's an effective way to drive change. Teams end up experiencing higher levels of authenticity when they buy in. I know I feel more authentic leading that way. So, I feel like as a leader, I can offer my best as I support the team."

Anastasia smiled warmly at Oscar. "Well, I can tell you that it's making a difference. Many of us on the team have talked about our experience this time around with Project One. Most are saying they've never felt this level of satisfaction. We are committed to delivering this project, which, considering how the first implementation failed, is pretty remarkable."

"I'm glad to hear that, Anastasia," Oscar said. "And thank you for that feedback about this being a positive experience. It reinforces what's possible if we continue on this path together."

Oscar felt his smart watch vibrate. As he glanced at his wrist, he said, "Hey, I have to head out in a couple of minutes to pick up my kids. Thank you for this wonderful chat and for sharing your story. I'm excited to see what we end up building together."

As they left the conference room, Anastasia noticed how energized the conversation made her feel. On her way back to her office, she thought about how she could bring some of these new change management practices to the HR team.

That week, knowing the team was on track, Oscar gave Diana the space to continue leading Project One while he shifted his attention to preparing for the follow-up board meeting. He planned to present his recommendation for creating an enterprise-wide approach to supporting the uncertain economic environment, and he hoped he could share good news about the upcoming Project One technology implementation.

13
Celebrate the Wins

THE FOLLOWING WEEK was critical for Project One as the team rolled out the first major technological enhancement. Diana and Lisa worked diligently to execute the agreed-upon communications strategy, operational readiness plans, and employee training. They devised several fun and engaging activities to educate and raise awareness around the improvements for both employees and customers. Informal positive feedback told them that staff recognized this approach as quite different from ABC's earlier change initiatives.

Feedback and user acceptance testing assured Diana that the new technology worked and other necessary pieces were in place. For her part, Lisa had confidence that the operations employees were looking forward to improved workflows and functions.

Their execution plans involved deploying the new technology in phases. For the first user group, the Project One leaders selected a small pilot team of high performers who were also among the most engaged employees. After training them on the production issues escalation protocol, most Project One team members removed themselves from the process. A few remained on standby to solve problems as necessary. When the first few days played out flawlessly, they breathed a collective sigh of relief.

After reviewing the team's early successes with Oscar,

Lisa authorized expanding to the next level of affected employees in the credit card customer service operations. Over the course of the next several weeks, they trained those employees on how to use the new technology.

When that cohort saw improved customer experience and efficiency immediately after implementation, many commented on how easy the new system was to use. Some even wondered aloud why they hadn't done it sooner.

Not one to let such a pivotal win slide by unnoticed, Oscar praised the Project One team and the employees involved in the rollout and documented early results in a company-wide email.

Oscar carried that excitement into his interactions with the committee tasked with developing ABC's enterprise approach to the ever-changing global trade developments, too. In particular, he shared his operations communications strategy as a starting point for the larger discussion around how to best scale and centralize core communications. It was essential, they knew, that all employees hear the same message and remain informed.

Though Oscar was the lead strategist for this effort, the committee unanimously agreed that Farouk's human resources team should own the plan since HR had responsibility for the employee experience, and they were in the best position to monitor employee sentiment. The corporate communications department would support the effort by crafting all messaging for Farouk's input and final approval.

Oscar and Farouk presented the plan at the next board meeting. "Erik, Michael, and members of the board, you asked this committee to develop an enterprise communication strategy around the shifting global trade situation. We'd like to walk you through our recommendations. Farouk will explain the plan we think makes the most sense," Oscar said.

Pleased with the committee's progress, Farouk, the chief human resources officer, was enthusiastic as he outlined their recommendations. "This strategy is one of the most comprehensive I've seen during my time at ABC," he began. "First, it includes approaches for planned and ad hoc communications from Michael to the entire organization. The ad hoc communications will be driven by any new information we need to share with staff.

"Michael's messaging will focus on remaining true to ABC's mission while recognizing uncontrollable changes outside the organization. We will equip leaders throughout the company with a set of FAQs that my team continually updates as needed. In addition, we will add a 'Global Tariff Situation' form on our intranet homepage that employees can use to submit questions or concerns. This will allow us to monitor potential rumors or misinformation.

"We'll share themes we identify from the concerns raised with a small group of senior leaders who will determine any next steps, including system-wide communication, that might be necessary. Their authority allows them to both identify actions and assign execution to staff. We recommend that each member of the executive team assign one of their direct reports to this group," he said.

Farouk sipped his coffee before continuing. "We will share concerns, action steps, and eventual resolutions at leadership meetings and employee town halls. Our primary goal with this new process is engaging employees in a dialogue rather than just talking at them. By publicly discussing what comes through this channel, we hope employees see that their voices are heard and their concerns are taken seriously."

"I like that, Farouk. It sounds like something we should've considered a long time ago," Michael said.

Farouk smiled at him and turned to the rest of the group as he continued.

"In addition to focusing on ABC's mission, Michael's messaging will reinforce the importance of clarity and focus. We realize the trade war can be a distraction. But the real concern we are hearing from employees is about ABC's financial position, which is not secret, and how a trade war could force us out of business. That's what we want to proactively get ahead of. Otherwise, rumors and speculation have the potential to really disrupt how employees feel about going to work every day. In other words, we are being preemptive here. And I'll steal Oscar's words about how we are leading with compassion rather than responding from fear. So, we want to get ahead by making resources available to help employees deal with any rising levels of stress or anxiety, no matter what the cause.

"Beyond access to ABC's confidential employee assistance program that includes resources for mental health concerns, we'll make available local organizations that can offer in-person and virtual classes on therapies that include meditation and breath work at no cost to employees. We're also thinking about offering a pre-recorded guided meditation call during lunch time every day," Farouk said.

Oscar made these suggestions to the committee after personally experiencing the power of innovative breathing techniques. He has also been meditating regularly for years. He credits much of his personal and leadership transformation to embracing these tools for reducing stress and increasing self-awareness. Most importantly, he leverages these techniques as part of his regular practice, rather than as a response strategy. That's why he doesn't always experience stress and anxiety the way that most do.

Robert, the CFO, asked, "Does setting all of this up involve costs that aren't already in the budget?"

"The additional costs are minimal," Farouk

acknowledged. "Oscar has relationships with a few local service providers who said they'll offer special group rates."

"We can use some of our existing technologies to support doing this at scale, too," Lora, the technology leader, added.

Pleased with the response, Robert smiled at Farouk and nodded for him to continue.

Farouk quickly scanned his notes before turning to the committee, "I think that is the gist of our recommendations. Did I miss anything?"

Several committee members commented that he had covered everything.

Farouk then turned to the larger group and said, "I'd like to open up the discussion for any questions or concerns." As Oscar observed silence and smiles, he knew that Farouk's thorough update was well-received.

Erik drew his seat closer to the long conference table and said, "I think this committee did a great job. The strategy seems very well-thought-out. I do have a couple of questions. Who owns this — one of you, or someone on your staff? And how will we know if these efforts are successful?"

"My team is in the best position to take ownership, Erik," Farouk replied. "Human resources is ultimately responsible for ABC's employee experience and well-being. I've already had a discussion with my chief of staff about making room for this, so she will do the heavy lifting on coordinating across the organization. Also, the committee discussed leading and lagging indicators that will correlate to employee sentiment. We have employee satisfaction, retention, and other key performance indicator measurements that we can collate to create a dashboard. My team already has access to and monitors that data.

"Lastly, we can use our existing survey capabilities to

do periodic pulse polls. We don't want to tax everyone with frequent surveys, so we'll take random samples that represent a good cross section of the organization. That would probably be our best measurement tool because we can gear the questions specifically toward the global trade situation and how it impacts the way employees feel about ABC, job security, and so on."

"This is well-planned, Farouk, and all of you on the committee. I feel good about how you're thinking about this," Erik said. "Anyone else from the board have concerns or questions? What about the executive team?"

"I think your team has done an impressive job, Farouk," Michael said, smiling at him. "Thank you."

There was a chorus of "Great jobs" and "Nicely dones" from most of the others in the room.

"I think we are good, so please start executing this strategy right away, Farouk," Erik said. "Are there any other orders of business before we conclude the meeting?"

"I do want to provide one update on Project One," Oscar replied. "The executive team is aware that we achieved a significant milestone with our first major implementation, and I'd like to share that here. I'm excited to report that all employees in the credit card customer service operations are using the new technology. The rollout across so many people was flawless. We owe a special thanks to the brilliance of Lora and her team. This technology is truly a game changer. We are seeing the efficiency gains in real time, which is exciting. Early indications are the customers are having a better experience, as well, because of the new self-service capabilities. I expect to have hard data to share at the next executive committee meeting," he added.

Obviously pleased, Erik replied, "That's wonderful news, Oscar! Congratulations! And well done, Lora! It sounds like things might be looking up, after all."

"Thank you, Erik," Lora beamed. "So far, we feel good

about what we've delivered and how we've delivered it. Diana has really taken charge, and she and Lisa have been great partners on the operations side. I'm optimistic, but I don't want to get too far ahead of ourselves. We have some smaller implementations in Lisa's credit card customer service area over the next few months before shifting our efforts to operations under Oscar. Some of those have nuanced complexities. But we have a solid plan and a strong team. I'm confident we'll continue to deliver at a high level," she concluded.

"I agree with everything you said," Oscar confirmed with a big smile.

"Well, let's keep our momentum going," Erik replied. "Thank you all for your time, and keep up the good work."

Oscar remained in the executive boardroom after everyone left and reflected on his early conversations with Farouk and Lora when he first joined ABC. Farouk had confided that, for some time now, he felt that HR wasn't truly valued. And Lora felt the technology department's strategic capabilities weren't fully leveraged.

Today was more about raising awareness of Farouk and Lora's leadership than it was about Oscar orchestrating the enterprise trade response strategy or delivering on Project One. The real wins were for Farouk, who presented a solution that could create a real benefit to the organization during a time that felt tumultuous, and for Lora, who was being seen as a strategic technology executive.

Oscar was by no means a glory hog. He was comfortable enough with himself to recognize that Farouk and Lora were both good leaders who deserved praise. Plus, a confidence boost and enhanced leadership visibility benefited them and the entire organization. While he had had good relationships with both since his first week, Oscar was now sensing a new strategic alliance beginning to form among the three. Giving the spotlight to the other two would help build trust. Without that, it would be nearly impossible for the executive team to improve its alignment and begin performing at a higher level.

Oscar's role was as the catalyst, not the star.

14
Success Builds Momentum

With support from Oscar, Lora and the other committee members worked with Farouk's HR team to quickly build out the committee's plan for organizational communications related to global trade and its impact on ABC's financial stability. They wanted to be careful about how much emphasis they placed on the outside distractions, lest employees lose focus on the company's mission.

Two months after executing the plan, Michael asked Farouk to report on its effectiveness at the upcoming executive team meeting. Oscar would also be updating the group on Project One. With all credit card customer service implementations completed and Diana preparing to establish a new team to start work on another business unit's customer service operations, the time was right.

Michael started the meeting by outlining his agenda. "Good morning, everyone. I'd like to spend as much of our time here as possible on two updates. The first is our progress with the enterprise communications strategy we put in place at the board's request, around employee concerns with the global trade situation's impact on ABC's longevity. The other update is about Project One. Then we can discuss any walk-in items anyone may have. Let's get started. Farouk, I'll turn the meeting over to you."

"Thanks, Michael," Farouk began. "I am pleased with

the communications plan results over the past few months. As you know, the administration recently announced higher than originally anticipated tariffs with some of the country's global trade partners. But even leading up to that outcome, there hasn't been much noise coming from employees during the past few weeks.

"We see this as a win. When we first rolled out the plan, we provided a way for everyone to ask questions and raise issues. And, we received *a lot* of input. As you all know, many questions were answered in our town halls and team meetings. That helped us resolve issues promptly and stop the rumors," Farouk said.

"What's interesting to see now is how this new communication channel opened a different, and quite productive, two-way dialogue between employees and senior leaders. We saw questions moving from concerns about global trade and ABC's financial solvency to other types of day-to-day challenges. It generated conversations about other lingering issues that people were concerned about. No matter what the topic, my HR team used the well-defined approach outlined in the original plan to prioritize and assign owners. Those people, in turn, did what was necessary to resolve those issues as much as possible.

"Of course, we haven't always been able to tell employees what they want to hear," Farouk continued. "But the leadership team's responsiveness and transparency continue to generate a lot of goodwill with employees across the organization.

"I know we all like to be able to measure progress, too, and I'm happy to report that this improvement is showing up in our latest employee satisfaction poll, which closed last week. We are in the early stages of analyzing the data, but I can say that our scores on questions related to communication, transparency, and trust in senior leaders are up across the board, which is promising."

"I know it's early, but how much of an improvement have we seen?" Michael asked.

"It's pretty significant," Farouk replied. "There is about a 2,500 basis-point improvement from last year's results on questions related to senior leadership transparency and trust."

"Wow!" Michael said, clearly impressed. "I don't think we've ever seen that big of a jump in those areas during my time as CEO here."

"It gets better," Farouk said, smiling. "We're using AI to analyze survey comments, and we've already noticed that people are saying they feel heard. Many are also commenting about how they've noticed we're resolving existing issues sooner and getting ahead of other concerns before they become bigger problems. They're noticing a positive change in our proactivity, and they appreciate it."

Oscar smiled as he listened to Farouk's update. He knows that a proactive approach to employee concerns can keep them from getting out of control. He's seen leaders elsewhere operate from fear when key issues were raised, sometimes because they were worried about long-term repercussions or being held accountable for something they had no control over. A proactive approach allows more room to operate with compassion. It also makes it possible for them to work with employees to fully understand any potential challenges while illuminating the risks that come with not addressing them early. Oscar knows that truly listening to employees helps create goodwill. And, delivering solutions only strengthens the relationship between leaders and staff. It's a strategic approach to building trust.

"There's one last theme we are seeing in the comments," Farouk continued. "In general, employees seem to appreciate the new mindfulness tools we introduced with local organizations. They feel better equipped to deal with not only what is happening at ABC, but also what's happening in their personal lives. Kudos to Oscar for suggesting those services."

Oscar smiled as Farouk continued.

"All in all, we're pleased with the results of the new communications strategy," he summarized. "I've been talking with my team about how we can institutionalize this, too. My question to everyone here is whether a few members from each of your teams can continue to triage and resolve other issues that come up. My guess is that over time, the number of issues will continue to trail off. And, when we experience other big changes, we should expect to see increased activity. Plus, we'll have what we need to respond in place already."

Lora was the first to respond. "I think it's a great process, Farouk. Consider my team onboard for ongoing support."

Phillip, Robert, and even Bijal, ABC's chief risk officer, agreed to make this communications strategy a standard practice.

"You have my support as well, Farouk," Oscar added.

An enthusiastic Farouk replied, "Great! I'll be sure to share this with my leaders and come back to you all with a more formalized plan on how we keep this process in place and running smoothly."

"Excellent, Farouk. Thank you," Michael said. "Oscar, let's get your Project One update now. I heard good things about it during last week's employee recognition luncheon."

Oscar flipped through his notes quickly before saying, "Thanks, Michael. We have hit a few key milestones for Project One. First, we have rolled out the new technology to all of Lisa's credit card customer service operations employees. This means all customer-facing and back-office employees in that unit are using the new platform. Most feedback from staff has been overwhelmingly positive because we have streamlined some manual processes, and the new AI-supported workflows allow people to navigate the system more easily. However, as with all change, there are pockets of people who would have preferred to stay on the old systems. And it's not because the old systems are better. In most cases, it's because they are reluctant to change and learn something new.

"I get it," he continued. "Change is hard. Many have significant tenure and simply like things the way they are. It's not a big problem — I'm just raising it so you're aware. I've never seen a scenario where there is 100% agreement on any change. Lisa's leaders are working with this group to understand and remove some barriers to change," he explained.

"On another positive note, since the launch, we have done several customer satisfaction surveys and are already seeing increases in overall satisfaction and our Net Promoter Score," he continued. "And, the number of customer follow-up calls, a key cost metric, is down significantly. The combination of self-service capabilities and improved customer workflows is reducing the number of calls generated while leading to better first-call resolution, too. In a few months, J.D. Power will publish the Credit Card Satisfaction Study results, and we're hoping our improved performance is reflected in our standing. We had our worst showing last year when we ranked twelfth. I might be overly optimistic, but during the next year, I predict we'll crack the top five again. We haven't been ranked that high in more than a decade. Our reimagined service experience is something I believe could establish a new benchmark in the industry," he said.

"Congratulations, Oscar! The initial performance improvements are very promising," remarked Robert.

"I know my team in finance is working with you on the realized cost savings from Project One. Can you shed some light on what we might expect to achieve based on where we are now?"

"I thought you might ask that, Robert," said Oscar, smiling. "First, on the technology side, there are significant financial benefits in our total cost of ownership from decommissioning old legacy systems and eliminating redundancies. Correct me if I'm wrong, Lora, but aren't we ahead of plan?"

"Yes, that is correct, Oscar. The cost reduction benefit is larger than originally anticipated," Lora replied.

Oscar continued, "Thanks, Lora. I also want to discuss the savings we expect from eliminating customer service positions. The business plan outlines a 35% reduction in credit card customer service staff. With that in mind, I'd like to propose something that might seem a bit unorthodox."

"Unorthodox in what way, Oscar?" Michael asked, intrigued, as a couple of others shifted in their seats.

"I did a little digging into how ABC manages layoffs. I learned that it's similar to what I've seen with other firms. However, one company that is similar to ours, because of its highly tenured workforce and close-knit culture, struggled for years to recover from significant staff cuts. There was such a grieving process from the layoffs that employees began to lose trust in leadership. Unfortunately, some key elements of the company's culture unraveled over time.

"Now, in fairness, that company's layoffs were unexpected. So, employees felt blindsided. Lisa's teams are aware there will be layoffs, but they aren't sure how deep those cuts will be. What I'd like to do is provide more transparency to the staff rather than simply going through with a chainsaw. ABC has a special culture, so I think it's important that we honor the staff contributions that got us to where we are today. Lisa and I discussed a potential solution that, with a little coordination, could minimize the damaging effects of the layoffs," Oscar said.

He continued, "First, we have some high performers in Lisa's operations, and we have a multitude of open positions in other parts of the organization that we need to fill. Working with HR, we'd like to assess the requirements for those roles and see where there might be overlap with our customer service employees' skills. In situations where there could be a good match, I'd like us to consider those in customer service operations who are losing their jobs before we look externally."

"We'd initially let interested customer service employees apply before we post the job requisition," Farouk added.

"Yes, that's one way to handle it, Farouk," Oscar replied. "Certain jobs would be open to customer service employees only. We would execute the process like a job redeployment, but candidates would be chosen based on merit and interviews. And this is only based on us having interested and able candidates. For jobs that aren't a good skills match, which we'll know quickly from our preliminary analysis, we continue with business as usual. Any jobs we don't fill with qualified customer service employees would go back to the usual process. With the right communications plan and dedicated resources to support interviews and candidate selection, I think we can fill some open roles in a matter of a few weeks," Oscar explained.

"It's an aggressive timeline, but I think we could manage," Farouk observed.

"I agree it would be an aggressive plan," Oscar replied. "It will require some real focus. But it's a critical activity to complete before the workforce reduction. If we create internal mobility for our higher performers who are ready for broader responsibility, we reduce the number of employees that we lay off. This approach can get us to the target 35% credit card customer service staff reduction while minimizing the impact on employees. Offering internal mobility also helps reduce some costs associated with training, employee onboarding, and so on. When I speak to the customer service staff about this approach, I have to explain this with full transparency.

"Oh, and one last thing. Once we know exactly how many credit card customer service employees we need to eliminate, I'd like to offer people a chance to volunteer to leave," Oscar added.

Several executives looked surprised by this statement.

Michael broke the awkward silence. "I'm not sure I'm comfortable with that, Oscar," he said.

"Can you tell me why?" asked Oscar.

"We've never done that before. And what if we get too many volunteers?" Michael replied.

He didn't want to admit it, but Michael thought that a willingness to leave might suggest that people didn't like working at ABC. He couldn't help but see that as a reflection of his leadership.

"That is definitely a risk, Michael," Oscar agreed. "But we could put a cap on it. And volunteering wouldn't guarantee a severance package. We would work with HR to develop selection criteria, and we'd be fully transparent about it. Asking for volunteers gives employees power to choose, which is better than feeling like the company doesn't want them.

"Everyone in this room knows cuts will improve ABC's health, but being told your job is eliminated can feel personal, especially when that isn't the intent. I mentioned there are pockets of individuals who don't agree with the changes we've made. I've talked to my team about how those resisting Project One changes end up creating resistance in the workplace. That isn't healthy for anyone, especially because it brings the people around them down.

If those individuals choose to leave, and that's quite possible, they can find a new employer where they will feel more aligned," Oscar explained.

"The communications plan rollout gave us an opportunity to get in front of this to help people make informed decisions. This staff cut is another opportunity for that. We have folks who are retirement-eligible or close to it. I can think of a couple of customer service employees who want to go back to school and pursue something else. How do we equip them to make that kind of decision? How do we prepare them to have conversations with their families so they can plan accordingly? We can provide resources to help people make a thoughtful choice and transition with much more ease.

"Our severance packages offer financial payouts, healthcare, and job placement support benefits that are generous, especially when compared to others in this industry. This presents an opportunity for us to work compassionately with employees on their transitions. And I'd like to suggest we do something other than blanket cuts. We need to analyze the impact. And it may cost us a little more financially. But I believe this is the type of scenario where both the exiting and remaining employees won't forget how we handled this," Oscar explained.

Robert frowned. "I'm not sure that's wise, Oscar. Financially, we're in dire straits here. We need all the help we can get," he replied.

Michael, who was warming up to the idea, tried to ease the sudden tension. "Let's talk about this before dismissing it out of hand, Robert. It's different from how we've handled workforce reductions in the past, and I'm intrigued. Farouk, do you have any concerns from a human resources perspective?"

Farouk thought for a moment before replying, "I can't think of any, Michael. This would be a new approach for us, but I have to say I like how intentional it is. It really puts employees first, and from an HR perspective, that's rarely a bad thing."

Oscar added, "If it's any consolation, Farouk, I know a smaller firm that followed a similar approach for necessary staff reductions, and it went surprisingly well. I have some thoughts on how we could execute this end-to-end. I suggest we bring Lisa into the discussion along with one of your senior HR leaders. Anastasia has been involved in Project One, so I think she could be very helpful with this."

"I agree, Oscar," Farouk said. "If you're okay with us exploring this, Michael, I can take the lead by developing a playbook and timeline to execute both the internal mobility process and staff reductions."

"If neither of you have concerns, I'm on board," Michael concluded. "I know time is of the essence, but let's review your playbook at our next executive meeting. It looks like we are almost at the top of the hour. I've got another meeting in a few minutes, so let's adjourn for now. Great work by everyone. We are creating momentum on many fronts. Let's keep it going."

During the next week, Oscar, Farouk, Lisa, and Anastasia met several times to map out a robust plan to establish a new protocol for layoffs that would also help them find new roles for high-performing customer service employees. After answering questions about it at the next executive committee meeting, they got the green light to move forward. It was a huge win for Oscar as he worked to bring more authenticity to the company's leadership and policies.

15
Lessons Learned

THE DAY AFTER the executive committee meeting, Diana and Oscar met to discuss lessons learned from the Project One implementations. They agreed to meet at Patisserie et Mes Amies, which had become Diana's favorite hideaway for working remotely after Oscar introduced her to it. She was already seated at Oscar's favorite corner table when he arrived.

"Hey, good afternoon, Diana. I see you've already secured my favorite spot," Oscar said, smiling.

"Yes, sir! Andres and his staff know this is *my* favorite table when you're not here, too," Diana replied, laughing.

"I'll have to ask Andres about reserving this table only for me," Oscar joked.

"I ordered a latte a few minutes ago. Do you want anything?" Diana asked.

"No, I'm good. I've had enough caffeine to power me for the rest of the week already," Oscar replied. "How about we go ahead and get started?"

"Sure," Diana said. "I know you wanted to discuss lessons learned from the first wave of Project One implementations. With that in mind, I met with the project team earlier this week to get their input on what went well and what they saw as opportunities for improving our change management process going forward. I will incorporate their feedback into this next phase as we begin working with the mortgage customer service operations group."

"That sounds like a good plan. What are some of the themes they brought up?" Oscar probed.

"Well, on the positive side, it was obvious the team felt very encouraged by the new change management process. Your coaching and guidance demonstrated that we had executive support. Going through the process-mapping exercises turned out to be very powerful for them. They never really thought about how each of them had a different understanding of how our processes actually work. That, in turn, informed how they felt about what we're changing and why. In the past, those differences created a lot of tension. Once we learned to not only accept, but embrace those differences, the tension dissipated and we worked in a very complementary way."

Diana paused as the server, Danielle, placed a latte in front of her.

"Anything for you, Oscar?" Danielle asked.

"Not now, but I might check out the pastry case before I leave," Oscar replied, smiling.

Diana thanked Danielle, then continued. "A few team members mentioned they began to feel more creative after a couple of design sessions. They saw that by learning to appreciate everyone's perspective, there was less judgment, so they began feeling safe enough to offer more progressive ideas. Lastly, by the end of this phase, they noticed they had significantly more trust in each other. They even trusted Lena from risk!" Diana laughed.

"Honestly, I believe these are all reasons why we will overachieve on our financial commitments," she continued. "They identified only two opportunities for improvement. First, they would've liked to have had a primer or training session on what to expect with the new change management process. Several people mentioned feeling uncomfortable going through the experience in real time without having more context. Second, they believe the organization would benefit from using this framework more broadly with all changes in various departments or functions. I'm not sure if it's feasible, but I think institutionalizing this approach is a great suggestion," Diana concluded.

"Very good," Oscar said. "Anything you would add personally?"

"Not really. They said what I was thinking, which felt validating, to be honest," Diana replied.

"Let me frame my question a different way," Oscar said. "When we met early in my tenure to discuss relaunching Project One, we talked a lot about authenticity and the change management framework. Do you have any observations or thoughts considering where we began this journey? What leadership lessons have you personally learned? I'm even more interested in that."

Diana sipped her latte as she thought about how to answer him.

"Actually, I do want something to snack on while we chat," Oscar said, standing up. "Let me go grab something. Think about those questions for a moment. They're important because there are some meaningful leadership lessons hidden in the incredible work you've delivered. I'll be right back!"

Reviewing her notes from earlier conversations with Oscar gave Diana a few ideas about the types of insights he was referring to. Before she knew it, he was back at his seat, taking the first bite from a caramelized sugar-crusted pastry called a kouign amann.

"All right," he began while using his napkin to wipe pieces of the flaky pastry from his lips. "Any thoughts come to mind?"

"Yes," Diana said confidently. "I remembered several of our early talks about authenticity and the change management framework, and can see how I've evolved as a leader by delivering the framework and observing the project participants."

"What do you mean?" Oscar asked, taking another bite.

"You caught me off guard, so I'm still trying to organize my thoughts. But let me share how I think about the lessons I got from my experience with the team. They fall into three categories: the framework, leadership, and stakeholders," Diana began.

"Okay, I like where this is going already," Oscar smiled, brushing crumbs off his lap.

"One of the first things you implied when you introduced the framework was the importance of context. You mentioned spending your first 90 days here developing context. You didn't want to make changes too quickly. You also said people's authenticity changes based on context. And when we were designing the first iteration of new processes, we discussed how, when the context changes, the next design iteration leads to a different solution. All that leads me to believe that context really matters. Solutions aren't one-size-fits-all. The state of the business, plus employee attitudes and experience, all influence what and how we create change."

A very pleased Oscar smiled broadly while Diana continued.

"The change management framework stages of awareness, acceptance, and assimilation are much more powerful than I thought. With your support, I was able to lead the teams through these phases. Our traditional change management tools fit well into those phases. What I found amazing is how these phases also applied to changes in my personal life. For example, a few months ago, I decided to move, partly because where I lived didn't excite me anymore. I sold my house in the suburbs and moved to the city. Acceptance, which was by far the hardest phase for me, required me to tackle some deeply rooted beliefs about stability symbols and the dream of home ownership. But I had to, because I wanted more flexibility and to be in a more socially vibrant area. It took some time to adjust, but I finally feel like I have completely assimilated into my new lifestyle. I'm used to my new commute, have met fun new neighbors, and I've developed entirely new social routines.

"The Project One team went through all these phases, as well," she continued. "We communicated early and often, raising awareness of why the project was important. Doing the current- and future-state process mapping eventually got the team to a place where members could accept both our current reality and where we are headed. Once we rolled out the new technology and trained everyone, they assimilated into the new environment, too. And now the context has changed for them."

"You're on a roll!" Oscar exclaimed. "What's next?"

"The last lesson in the framework category is about resonance and resistance. By the way, I hope you don't mind, but I have renamed these 'the quantum effect,'" Diana explained.

"Oh, that's fancy," Oscar said enthusiastically. "Tell me more."

Diana gladly continued. "Resonance and resistance are all about energy. You can't see them, but they are there. And we feel them through things like emotions. To steal your words, we must get enough energy in resonance for change to happen. On the flip side, resistance stops change from happening.

"Those are the three framework category lessons. Any questions before I move on to leadership, which is the next lesson category?" she asked.

Oscar shook his head no.

"For leadership, I observed you and how you helped anchor and align us. When you took a step back and allowed me to lead, I found myself demonstrating some of the same leadership behaviors as you. The first was helping us integrate perspectives. You had a way of honoring what brought us to the present before introducing new ways of thinking. And bringing those two sides together was powerful. You were new to ABC, but you didn't tell us all the things we were doing wrong, which, to be honest, was what we half expected. Your point of view was 'How do we build from here?' I know for a fact that we all appreciated your humility and lack of judgment," Diana said, smiling, before continuing.

"The next leadership lesson is adaptability. When things didn't go according to plan or our expectations, you didn't invest much energy in the obstacles. You moved like water onto the next set of possibilities. We simply pivoted and kept moving forward.

"You often talk about alignment, and the word I use to describe this next lesson is 'connection.' From the very beginning, you helped everyone on the team see the connection to ABC's bigger mission. I've been reading about how alignment is so important to employees that those who feel more aligned with their organization's purpose are willing to accept less money or fewer benefits. And it's because there is a connection between them and some higher organizational purpose. You helped us stay focused on the bigger picture and the company's greater good. That led to us dealing with fewer ego and personality conflicts. No one put their own interests above the company's or those of our customers and employees," she said as she tipped her head back to get the last of her latte.

"The next lesson is collaboration. And this may seem intuitive, but in my experience, just because people are on the same team doesn't mean they have collaboration on their minds. The Project One team members had genuine differences of opinion, and as we uncovered them, we offered each other compassion and empathy. We heard every voice. We accepted our differences and could work together, eventually becoming what I saw as a high-performing unit. This was a different type of collaborative effort. And you, leading with compassion, helped us achieve that.

"My last lesson under leadership is support. And I probably benefited the most from this. You knew exactly when to lead and when to turn things over to me. There was a wonderful balance. And the team and I knew that even when you weren't present in meetings, we could count on you for coaching and reinforcement later if we needed it. You made sure we celebrated our quick wins, which created momentum, rather than waiting until the very end of the project to recognize everyone's contributions. Many of us have never felt that type of support in our careers here. So, thank you for that," she concluded.

"Wow!" Oscar exclaimed. "I didn't realize you and the team noticed some of the less obvious things I was doing."

"Well, our typical approach has been that an executive wants us to deliver a project. We provide updates monthly, and when the project is completed, we are either praised or chastised. So, to feel your level of engagement and support was such a different experience," Diana replied.

Smiling warmly, Oscar said, "I'm glad it didn't go unnoticed."

Diana smiled back and continued. "There's just one more category, stakeholders. These are some of my observations, plus input from the team about how they experienced this highly authentic change-management approach. And I think of these as outcomes from everything I've mentioned related to framework and leadership.

"First, people felt safe with you. There was something about the way you showed up and the environment you created that led to psychological safety. Even during my second interaction with you when we met to discuss Project One, you very quickly made me feel safe. And that led to me feeling more authentic in how I approached our interactions.

"That increased safety also led to the team and me

feeling like we could trust you. And eventually, people on the team began trusting each other and themselves. With all the different opinions and perspectives being accepted, we understood there were no right or wrong answers, just different viewpoints. With no judgment, we learned to embrace that," she said.

"And because we developed so much momentum towards resonance rather than resistance, it seemed to require less energy to accomplish our tasks," Diana explained. "Yes, at times we worked long hours. But it didn't feel like work because we were so energized. This is a part of that 'quantum effect' I mentioned.

"Increased creativity is next. I'm pretty sure the high trust levels and psychological safety sparked our creativity. New ideas seemed to come out of nowhere. I think we developed some innovative solutions that we didn't even think were possible.

"The second-to-last lesson is mirroring behavior. I don't know if you noticed this, but I started using the language you introduced. A team member even mentioned that some of my mannerisms began to remind them of you. Clearly, I was mirroring your behaviors. And over time, they started to do the same. Instead of relying on you to help us build trust and create an environment that was safe and fostered creativity, we began building that ourselves. But you were the catalyst that gave us permission to show up this way."

Diana smiled at Oscar before making her last point. "Lastly, we became optimistic. We all know ABC has been in a tough financial position, and Project One is literally its savior. So, we've felt a lot of pressure to deliver. But once we started developing momentum, our optimism went through the roof. I didn't hear one person doubt our ability to deliver something valuable to the organization.

"There's one more thing that I'll mention quickly. I don't have it as a lesson, but it's something you told me early on. You said that fear always reduces authenticity. Regardless of how things were going, not once did you ever project fear towards me or the team. That was monumental in allowing us to continue toward our sense of authenticity. Even the concerns about a potential trade war could've been a much bigger distraction. But because you projected fearlessness and continued to operate with compassion, we felt we had the space to do the same.

"All right, I've said a lot. So, what do you think?" Diana finally asked.

"If I'm being honest," Oscar began. "I'm completely blown away. A former mentor used to always say, 'Talent is visible.' And I knew from our first interaction that you were talented. But your thoughtfulness around these experiences with Project One, which has been going on for almost a year now, is truly next level. I'm humbled by yours and the team's observations around my impact. It's always been my intention to create an environment like the one you've described. So, to hear it from you and to see the results, which will have a tangible impact on the company, is remarkable. I'm at a loss for words."

"Just by being a highly authentic leader, you have changed us, Oscar. And I for one am grateful and excited about what's next," Diana replied.

"The feeling is mutual, Diana," Oscar added. "And hey, I'd love to have a copy of your list. The team mentioned some sort of primer or training on the framework. Sharing some of this with the executive team could allow us to get support from our learning and development colleagues for this. I'm sure Farouk would be on board," Oscar said.

"And what a great way to end my week! Anything else you want to add before we get a start on the weekend?" he asked.

"No, I've shared everything I wanted to. Thanks for making the time, Oscar. I look forward to starting work with the mortgage customer service operations next week," Diana said, visibly grateful.

"I always enjoy our time together, Diana. And thank you for all the encouragement. It means a lot. Let's walk back to the office now. I'm going to head home shortly, and I hope you plan to, also," Oscar said.

Diana and Oscar waved goodbye to the staff and walked briskly back to ABC headquarters. Diana responded to a few emails and documented the three categories and lessons learned from the first phase of Project One before packing up for the weekend.

FIGURE 11. LESSONS LEARNED

THE FRAMEWORK

- **Context Matters** – No solution is free of context. Solutions are not one size fits all. Understanding the nuances of the environment and the stakeholders all matter when leading change.

- **Awareness, Acceptance and Assimilation** – These phases apply to all changes whether personal or professional.

- **The Quantum Effect (Resonance and Resistance)** – You need enough energy in resonance to create the change you desire. Resistance slows down and can even stop change from happening.

THE LEADERS

- **Integrating Perspectives** – An ideal solution honors what is and the journey the organization has been on while also bringing in new thinking. Knowing when to combine the new and the old is powerful.

- **Adaptability** – When things don't go according to plan, make changes and keep moving forward.

- **Connection** – Everyone innately wants to be connected to something bigger than themselves. Tying the change back to the mission or purpose helps create alignment.

- **Collaboration** – Embrace differences in how the world is seen while creating a shared vision of the future. Get others to a place of acceptance (which can be hard!).

- **Support** – Leaders offer coaching, positive reinforcement, and compassion rather than creating fear. They eliminate roadblocks and help to create momentum. They encourage celebrating success, especially the small wins.

THE STAKEHOLDERS

- **Psychological Safety** – People show up feeling more authentic in an environment that feels safe and is high in trust.

- **Energy Exertion** – When the team is feeling resonance, they use less energy. You don't have to work so hard.

- **Creativity** – When participants feel more authentic, there are higher levels of creative expression.

- **Mirroring** – The team modeled the behaviors of the highly authentic leader.

- **Optimism** – Building momentum reduced doubt about achieving the goal.

NOTE: Fear ALWAYS reduces authenticity

ଓଞ୍ଚ

Meanwhile, as he left early, Oscar looked forward to ending the week on another high with a special date night with his wife, Elena.

16
One More Date Night

"DO YOU WANT your usual from Kalaya?" Elena shouted upstairs to Oscar.

"Yes, please," Oscar replied from the bedroom as he changed out of his work clothes into something more comfortable for date night.

"Got it," Elena said, mostly to herself as she grabbed her cell phone to call their favorite Thai restaurant. Their usual was beet salad, yellow curry with chicken, drunken noodles, roasted spicy eggplant with mango, and sticky rice. It was a lot of food, even for a family of four. But everyone loved how the flavors melded over time into excellent leftovers. Oscar especially enjoyed the spicy eggplant the next day. Tonight's meal was just for two because the twins were at a sleepover.

Elena poured a glass of white wine for each of them as Oscar made his way downstairs into the kitchen.

"I'm ready," he said with a happy grin, pointing to his t-shirt and checkered flannel pajama pants.

"Those pants continue to be ridiculous," Elena replied with an eye roll before kissing her husband on the cheek. She handed him his wine. "I'm glad we decided to order in and watch movies tonight."

"Yes, we both had long weeks. How long until the food gets here?" Oscar asked.

Elena took a sip of wine before replying, "45 minutes or so. Let's catch up while we wait. I want to hear the latest and greatest about what's happening at ABC. I know you were excited about some of the recent milestones."

"Good idea," Oscar replied, leading the way to the sunken family room adjacent to the kitchen. "It was a very rewarding week."

"I'm so glad. Tell me more," Elena said, taking a seat close to Oscar on the couch.

He let out a long, relieved sigh. "Well, as you know, the first phase of Project One is now complete. Diana and the team did an excellent job of implementing the new technology in the credit card customer service operations. Our customers and most of our employees are responding favorably. And we are pretty confident that we'll surpass what we promised for cost savings. That will begin to put ABC in a much better position in terms of financial sustainability.

"Diana is pulling together a new team for this next phase, which will do the same thing for the mortgage customer service operations. With so much early success, I've challenged her to consider whether we can also run a parallel project workstream for another business operation — like retail or investment banking customer service — at the same time. This would help accelerate some of the benefits," he said.

"That's amazing! It's hard to believe you have been at ABC for not quite a year, and you've already made such an incredible mark. I'm so proud of you!" Elena exclaimed.

"Thank you," Oscar replied, blushing. "That means a lot. To be fair, we still have a ways to go before we are out of the woods and in a better financial position. But we have momentum. Technology aside, I'm mostly impressed with how the Project One team functioned. Everyone embraced the change management framework I taught Diana to use as part of this. Yes, I coached and supported her and the team. But I have been very impressed with Diana's leadership. When we met today to discuss lessons learned from the first phase, she told me about the deeper leadership lessons she either experienced or observed from the team and me. Her awareness level and openness are truly exceptional. In a very short period, she has transformed her leadership approach and seen such positive results," Oscar said.

"How much do you think working with you has to do with that?" Elena asked.

"You know, I've always seen myself as a catalyst for change and for increasing authenticity in others," Oscar began. "But I've never seen this level of transformation in a leader happen so quickly. And I recognize that it is Diana's openness to new ways of thinking and working that's creating these results. So, it's not all me. In fact, it's mostly her. That has me thinking about the true potential of leading through change and increasing authenticity on a broader scale at ABC, too. It makes me hopeful about what I might be allowed to help build there. The question, though, is around how I can find more Dianas. And, how does Diana engage with other leaders in a way that opens them up to a new approach, as well?"

"The good old locks and keys, right?" Elena smiled.

Oscar laughed and clinked his glass against Elena's. "Cheers to that," he said before continuing.

"In addition to Project One's success, the organization has really improved communication between employees and senior leadership. The new processes and tools we rolled out to get ahead of the tariff noise have been embraced across the organization. Farouk, our head of HR, recently recommended in an executive update that we make this our standard practice. I can't tell you how rewarding that is. This solution began as my brainchild, and I'm beginning to feel like it has the potential to touch and influence so many more in the organization. ABC has a great culture, but it needs to evolve if we want to stay relevant. And I feel like I can help lead us to a different place with some of these wins.

"You remember, Michael, the CEO, right?" When Elena nodded, Oscar continued.

"He used to be hesitant about acting on some of my ideas. And who can blame him? I was the new guy — and one he didn't handpick — and I was unproven as far as he was concerned. Now, he warms up much more quickly. And several on the executive team are beginning to connect with me more often. Lora, our CTO, has been a key partner with Project One. I love collaborating with her. She is so brilliant! Lora and Phillip, our chief growth officer, asked to meet with me next week to discuss an idea around a technology project they think could create and deliver an innovative new product. I'm curious to see what the two of them have been brainstorming.

"But," Oscar paused while taking another sip of wine, "as you'd imagine, not everyone is signing up for my fan club."

"Really?" Elena gasped in sarcastic shock.

"Nope," Oscar grinned. "There are still people who want to stay true to the old way. I understand it. And it's natural. People like our CFO, Robert, or Bijal, the chief risk officer, have succeeded at ABC by doing what the company has always done. And there was a time when that served the organization well.

"I appreciate Robert's conservative financial acumen, which works well when the industry is growing and profit margins are high. But times are different, and because he vetoed important technology and product investments before, ABC hasn't grown as much as it could have. And Bijal? He successfully led ABC through a great deal of regulatory change ten years ago. But the regulatory environment is more relaxed under the current government administration, which gives us opportunities for taking a little more risk with our strategy and resulting decisions. My point is that I truly honor their contributions. But I wonder whether they're the right people to help us get through the next five years," he said, frowning.

"Since you're not in Michael's shoes as CEO, what will you do?" Elena asked.

"I'll continue to value their perspectives and help them understand where we might be able to make more aggressive decisions," Oscar said. "And I think the goodwill I have built with Michael, Erik, and the board adds to the change momentum we have already. Plus, with leaders like Farouk, Lora, and Phillip leaning in and aligned with the idea of a different approach, one that should lead to greater financial stability, I think Michael will have to think long and hard about the dynamics across the executive team. At least if I were in his position, I'd be thinking about that. We will see how it all plays out."

"It sounds like you've got it all figured out, my dear," Elena softly encouraged. "If you are meant to help ABC continue to shift and change, I'm sure you will do your best to create those opportunities. And the right people to help will show up in the most unexpected ways. You know that's how the universe works."

"I sure do!" Oscar replied.

As they raised their glasses for another clink, the doorbell rang.

"Our dinner! Finally!" Oscar exclaimed.

After dinner, they settled back in on the couch, side by side and feet stretched out on the coffee table, to watch two Netflix movies. Date night wasn't flashy, but it was a relaxed and enjoyable way to start their weekend.

Over the course of the next two months, ABC continued to gain momentum with Project One's implementation. In addition, Oscar, Farouk, Lisa, and Anastasia completed all the playbook tasks that would help place the credit card customer service operations high performers who would lose their jobs into other positions in the company. Fortunately for ABC, most of the high performers who wanted to stay accepted new internal positions, which helped reduce the number of people let go. In addition, ABC provided career and retirement planning services to help others think through whether they wanted to stay or accept a severance package when one was offered.

As Oscar had anticipated, many of those who opposed Project One changes took the severance option. And some people ABC would have liked to have kept opted to leave because the financial payout allowed them to go back to school, or because they simply decided it was time for a career change. Others left because the severance deal provided what they needed to enjoy time off from any type of job, even temporarily. As a highly authentic leader who always put people first, Oscar was supportive and encouraging, no matter what option people chose. As far as he was concerned, there was no right or wrong decision. He knew that if people felt good about owning their decision, they would take that aligned energy into whatever they did next.

And, he was blown away by how many of the employees who were leaving stopped by his office to thank him. They recognized he was a different type of leader. They hadn't experienced the type of transparency and compassion Oscar offered before. A few said they knew he genuinely cared about both them and the corporation, something they weren't sure was possible until they experienced it with his leadership. Some told Oscar he was refreshingly authentic. They knew that if Oscar continued to lead with his most authentic self, ABC not only had a fighting chance for survival but would probably end up thriving.

In a very short period, Oscar had cemented himself in ABC's lore. With so much early success, the big question in Oscar's and everyone else's mind was, "What's next?"

Appendix
Organizational Profile

ANYWHERE BANKING CORPORATION (ABC) is a 75-year-old multinational banking and financial services firm based in the United States. The company operates through five business units offering diversified products and services for consumers and businesses:

1. Credit Card — Consumer and small business credit cards
2. Consumer Retail Banking — Deposit accounts, personal loans, auto loans, and mortgages
3. Business and Commercial Banking — Deposit, payment, and lending solutions for small, midsize, and large businesses
4. Investment Banking — Trading and securities, investment banking, and institutional lending
5. Asset Management — Investment management and brokerage services

ABC started as a consumer retail bank with a strong branch-banking presence in the Midwest. One of the first to launch a consumer credit card, it maintained a competitive advantage for many years by creating a best-in-class customer experience. By the late 1980s, ABC began expanding offerings by launching a suite of small business products and services.

After the 2008 financial crisis, organic growth slowed. With a strong cash position, the company began diversifying its service offerings and expanding its customer base by strategically acquiring brokerage and investment management firms.

ABC's strong culture leads to below-industry-average turnover and enables near-lifelong employment. Despite its scale, employees typically do not cross-pollinate, growing their careers within their specific business lines instead.

Thanks to limited investment in technology that has resulted in antiquated systems and processes, ABC is currently fighting for its survival. Because it has lost its competitive advantage as a customer experience industry leader, the board of directors is pressuring CEO Michael, a longtime employee and industry veteran, to redirect the ship. While his executive team is a mix of talented and highly skilled legacy ABC employees and newer leaders, Michael hasn't been able to get the most from them. This is most likely because the most influential executives, individuals who have worked together a long time, continue to rely on conservative decision-making that was successful in the past but doesn't work in the present environment.

Leadership Bios

Name: Erik
Title: Chair of the Board
Tenure: 5 years on board, 1 year as board chair
Education: BS Economics, MBA from Oxford University
Professional Background:
- Former CEO of a media conglomerate
- Experience working and investing in Silicon Valley, fintech, and manufacturing
- Board member of three other Fortune 500 companies

Key Beliefs:
- Environmental, social, and governance issues (ESG) are important
- Organizations must change to remain relevant
- Leadership starts at the top and "makes everything else go"

Name: Michael
Title: Chief Executive Officer
Tenure: 35 years at ABC, 6 as CEO
Education: BS Finance, MBA from The Wharton School
Professional Background:
- Grew up at ABC and rose through the organization via dealmaking in the company's investment banking unit
- Developed experience by leading global business units across consumer banking, business banking, and asset management
- Reputation for building strong relationships
- Sometimes comes off as a bit salesy

Key Beliefs:
- Relationships are key to getting things done
- Loyalty matters
- The future is always bright (highly optimistic)

Name: Oscar
Title: Chief Operating Officer
Tenure: Recently hired
Education: BA Philosophy, MBA from the University of Oregon
Professional Background:
- 25 years as a transformational leader with a strong foundation in financial services, but has led large-scale operations and other functions across multiple industries
- Strong focus on aligning people, process, and technology
- Developed a reputation as a general manager with broad experience who takes a systems view to solve problems

Key Beliefs:
- Authenticity is a core capability that all organizations can develop and leverage
- Working in a space where you can be who you are is critical to getting the best out of people
- Empowering people is a force multiplier for improving organizational performance

Name: Robert
Title: Chief Financial Officer
Tenure: 30 years at ABC, 5 as CFO
Education: BS Finance, CPA, MS Finance from the University of Delaware

Professional Background:
- Started as an auditor at a Big 4 accounting firm, where ABC was a client
- ABC recruited him to join staff
- Has followed Michael into different business units and been promoted accordingly
- Known as Michael's long-term right-hand guy

Key Beliefs:
- Relationships are key to getting things done
- Loyalty matters
- A conservative financial strategy is best

Name: Lora
Title: Chief Technology Officer
Tenure: 8 years at ABC, 3 as CTO
Education: BS Computer Science, MS Data Science from Northwestern University
Professional Background:
- Former CTO at a start-up fintech that went public; also has experience in large, established financial services firms
- Started career as a developer and began leading teams early due to high EQ and innate leadership skills

Key Beliefs:
- Technology can solve many organizational problems but requires strong buy-in from business partners to explore possibilities and help design solutions
- ABC is run by an old guard of leaders who don't really want to change

Name: Farouk
Title: Chief Human Resources Officer
Tenure: 7 years at ABC, 5 as CHRO
Education: BS Business Management, MA Organizational Development from Michigan State University, PhD Organizational Behavior from the University of Michigan
Professional Background:
- Former head of HR at a large global manufacturing firm
- First role at ABC was leading people strategy redesign, while having responsibility for global HR business partners

Key Beliefs:
- The people agenda often takes a backseat to financial motivations
- Feels under-utilized as an advisor to the executive team
- Is rarely consulted on strategic topics and would like to change that

Name: Bijal
Title: Chief Risk Officer
Tenure: 20 years at ABC, 5 as CRO
Education: BS Business Management, MS Enterprise Risk Management from Boston University
Professional Background:
- Spent entire career in financial services risk management and/or compliance roles

Key Beliefs:
- Managing risk has been paramount to the firm's historical success
- The organization must change incrementally due to ill-advised strategic initiatives of the past
- Strongest voice at the executive leadership table and has the CEO's support

Name: Phillip
Title: Chief Growth Officer
Tenure: 4 years at ABC, 3 as CGO
Education: BS Marketing, MBA from Columbia University
Professional Background:
- Former chief marketing officer for a large consumer bank
- Expert in designing digital capabilities and leveraging them to drive growth

Key Beliefs:
- ABC must solve internal challenges to grow
- The executive team is not aligned on organizational priorities
- Innovate by testing and learning

Name: Darren
Title: Head of Operations
Tenure: 25 years at ABC, 4 as Head of Operations
Education: BS in Engineering, MBA from the University of Texas
Professional Background:
- Began career at ABC in a frontline operations leadership role and progressed to leading global operations
- Strong familiarity across business lines; architect of the current operating model

Key Beliefs:
- He is the smartest person in the organization
- He has built an operational system that is at the forefront of the industry; it just isn't well-executed
- The operating model would fall apart if he weren't leading it, and that gives him leverage

Name: Diana
Title: Program Leader
Tenure: 10 years at ABC, 2 as Program Leader
Education: BS Business Management
Professional Background:
- Held a variety of operational subject matter expert roles in competitor companies before joining ABC
- Has moved quickly through operational leadership positions since joining ABC
- Made a name for herself by balancing operational expertise, leadership, and project delivery

Key Beliefs:
- She has the resilience to tackle any business challenge facing her
- Recognizes she has moved quickly in her career, but feels the organization has used her skills without truly giving her what she wants from the deal
- If she doesn't begin to feel more valued, she'll consider exploring outside opportunities

Name: Lisa
Title: Head of Credit Card Customer Service Operations
Tenure: 25 years at ABC, 7 as department head
Education: BS Hospitality Management, MBA from Cornell University
Professional Background:
- Began career at ABC in customer service right out of college
- Known as an advocate for people development and culture shaping
- Strong understanding of how technical aspects influence both employee and customer experiences

Key Beliefs:
- Because the executive team lacks alignment and continuity, both employees and customers suffer
- Strategic decisions are often short-sighted and don't involve the right level of input from key stakeholders
- In general, the organization doesn't hold leaders accountable